CREATIVE DANCE FOR BOYS

CREATIVE DANCE
FOR BOYS

by

Jean Carroll

and

Peter Lofthouse

MACDONALD & EVANS LTD.
8 John Street, London W.C.1
1969

First Published March 1969
©
MACDONALD & EVANS
1969

S.B.N.: 7121 0318 X

PRINTED BY Unwin Brothers Limited
THE GRESHAM PRESS OLD WOKING SURREY ENGLAND

Produced by letterpress

A member of the Staples Printing Group   (HL3083)

Preface

FOR many years both men and women teachers have been doing very successful work in creative dance with mixed classes in primary schools. Some women—and fewer men—have also worked successfully with older boys and men students. Development has been limited, however, by the general suspicion that creative dance is unsuitable for youths and men. Much of this suspicion stems from the traditional emphasis on games and athletics in boys' schools. A contributory factor has been that theatrical dance in this country has been dominated by classical ballet, so that, until recently, we have lacked an effective demonstration of dance at the professional level, in a virile contemporary idiom. This suspicion of dance was strengthened by an historical accident. Rudolf Laban and Lisa Ullmann came to Great Britain and worked with educationists in movement at a time when men physical educationists were in the forces. Many women physical educationists eagerly took up their ideas and began implementing them in schools and colleges.

When the men returned to civilian life they had not only missed the developments of the intervening six years, but had also had their minds focused on the military purposes of movement and these, inevitably, conflict with educational and artistic purposes. This led to an unfortunate division between men and women physical educationists, with both sides being responsible for a breakdown in understanding and communication. Fortunately, this situation is now improving rapidly, and the divergencies of approach to movement by men and women physical educationists are proving mutually enriching. This book is a product of such collaboration. Jean Carroll is responsible for the text, but the actual material has been discussed with and tested in boys' schools by Peter Lofthouse. Its purpose is to provide men teachers with an introduction to creative dance for boys.

Those aspects of movement which are most relevant educationally to boys between the ages of 10 and 16 years have been selected as a basis for the book. Each chapter takes an aspect of movement, places it within the

5

educational setting, and gives specific examples of its application, including descriptions of actual lessons taken with boys.

Chapter 1—deals with warming up and mobilising the class for expressive movement.

Chapter 2—is based on the appeal to boys of dynamic activities.

Chapter 3—concentrates on form and structure in expressive movement.

Chapter 4—explores relationship situations, and juxtaposes material that satisfies the need for individual work and material that satisfies the need for group experience.

Chapter 5—suggests different ways of challenging boys in creative dance and of ensuring progression.

We should like to express our warm appreciation of the co-operation of the headmasters, staff, and pupils of Walton Secondary Boys' School, Addlestone Secondary School and Ottershaw School. We should also like to acknowledge our gratitude to Miss Lisa Ullmann and Miss Olive Chapman, who read the text and made helpful suggestions, and Miss Elizabeth Mauldon, Miss Joy Mutlow and Miss Betty Redfern, who have all been kind enough to discuss aspects of the book with us. We are greatly indebted to Mr. Adrian Wood, who is responsible for the photographs.

J. C. and P. L.

January 1969

Contents

CHAPTER 1

Dance in the Education of Boys

THE very title of this book states a deliberate false premise. There is, in fact, no difference between the movement experience that is valuable for boys and that which is valuable for girls. The principles of movement formulated by Laban are principles of *human* movement. It would be nonsense to suggest that there is something called boys' dance which is fundamentally different from girls' dance—any more than there is boys' music and girls' music, boys' painting and girls' painting, boys' poetry and girls' poetry. As in these other media, there are, in movement, merely some different stresses within the same overall experience, so that we recognise that boys and girls often produce differently stressed answers and responses to the same problem or stimuli. Some of these stresses arise from the different physiological make-up of the sexes: others arise from the different social conditioning that boys and girls receive.

Even in our society, however, which is becoming more flexible, rôle cognitions and expectations cannot be neglected. They will most easily be experienced and used when dance is taught in mixed classes, and for a full exploration of the potential of dance as a medium both boys and girls should be engaged in it in mixed groups. In our schools there are still many situations, however, where boys have to be taught separately. No rational explanation of the value of dance or its significance in the curriculum will impress either them or their teachers, if, when they are plunged into their first experience of it, they are made to feel foolish or unmanly. The educational claims for dance, therefore, are based on the assumption that the actual material presented to boys will re-assure them of their masculine rôle when dancing.

"Art is not one of life's decorations. It is that which characterises man as man.

"It is a form of work, and work is an activity peculiar to mankind."*

* Ernst Fischer, *The Necessity of Art* (Pelican 1963) p. 15.

9

Ernst Fischer goes on to justify this striking assertion by claiming that "work is transformation of the natural." This transformation manifested itself originally in what Whitehead terms "ceremonial evolutions from which issue play, religious ritual, tribal ceremonial, dance, pictures on caves, poetic literature, prose, music."*

These manifestations in their contemporary forms are now, rightly, part of the educational programme, apart from dance, which in our particular society has been neglected and even distrusted. Other societies have, of course, managed to retain both dance and a conviction of the masculinity of their males. It seems misguided to leave out of the curriculum this one art form which has been a powerful means of expression throughout history.

"Basically concerned with the primary issues of life, dance has been inseparably connected with the expression of the cultural development of every period, and in turn has exerted its influence on the social patterns of the past."†

The place of the arts in education has been given enthusiastic recognition in most of our schools. For some children expression through words, sound or paint may present difficulties. Even those who can use these other media successfully often find great satisfaction in expression through movement. And for some children movement may be the medium, above all others, which allows them to fulfil their creative potential.

Dance is concerned with organising and coming to terms with, expressing and commenting on human experience. In these ways it is allied with the other art forms. But dance is also allied with gymnastics and games and athletics in the physical education programme. This, too, is perfectly under-standable, for dance is indissolubly linked with all these activities involving human movement. Gymnastics arises from the child's delight in using movement to grapple with problems of mastering the environment—of supporting his body in precarious balance, of leaping on to apparatus, of arriving safely on the floor from heights. Games arise from the child's delight in the skill of using implements to control moving objects such as balls, tops and quoits in competitive situations. Athletics arise from the child's delight in running, jumping and throwing in measurable situations. In swimming

* A. N. Whitehead, *Adventures of Ideas* (Pelican 1942) p. 312.

† Margaret N. H'Double, *Dance—A Creative Art Experience* (University of Wisconsin Press 1940) p. 46.

children experience movement in another physical element, and have to adjust themselves to the different demands that this makes. In all these activities movement is used operationally, to serve an external purpose—whether that purpose be scoring a goal, clearing a hurdle or swimming a length. Now, in dance, movement is used for the inner purpose of expression. Inner feelings or moods, direct observation of external reality or the act of moving in itself can provoke movement images, and these, in dance, are formulated in an artistic way that heightens and controls the initial raw experience.

The potential for response in dance is within all of us, and can be seen in the spontaneous movement of young children, but, because of inhibitions imposed by our particular social conditioning, the initial motivation to dance in school must be provided by the teachers. There is no competitive pressure to provide motivation as in games and athletics. How do we release this potential, especially in older boys where the inhibitions may be operating more powerfully? One way is obliquely: where Nuffield science and the "new maths" and personal writing are flourishing in a school, there should be the excitement and flexibility that will readily accept dance as a natural means of discovery and expression. However, the dance or physical education teacher must believe in and must adopt an approach that demonstrates the relevance of dance to the contemporary situation, and to the interests and problems and aspirations of individual boys.

The right attitude and convictions are essential to success, but these cannot be achieved except on a basis of understanding. Understanding can only come from an exploration of the meaningfulness of movement. This meaningfulness is outside the scope of words: it is, like mathematics, another language. The rest of the chapters of this book deal with specific situations and experiences of movement, which, it is hoped, will give teachers and boys some insight into and satisfaction from dance as a creative activity.

"In order to be an artist it is necessary to seize, hold and transform experience into memory, memory into expression, material into form. Emotion for an artist is not everything; he must also know his trade and enjoy it, understand all the rules, skills, forms and conventions. . . ."*

* Ernst Fischer, *op. cit.* p. 9.

11

The understanding of dance which this book is intended to promote is based on the classification formulated by Rudolf Laban. Laban saw movement as a universal phenomenon, and studied particularly the nature and significance of human movement. He was primarily concerned with the beneficial effects to be gained from participating in *Bewegungskunst*, an almost untranslatable term, to which "the art of movement" approximates. He enabled us to recognise different aspects in the complex phenomena of human movement and, simplified, these aspects are:

1. THE BODY: THE NATURE OF ITS MOVEMENT

The body itself, with its many parts, is the means by which human movement manifests itself. Physical educationists have always known a great deal about this, and have been able to answer, in detail, the question "What moves?" in any action.

2. EFFORT: HOW THE BODY MOVES

Whenever the body moves, its actions are impelled by energies—the neuro-muscular energies of thinking, feeling man. These impulses to move, and the resulting stresses they give to movement, Laban called "efforts." He discriminated between these efforts more systematically and thoroughly than anyone had done before. He differentiated between

firm, powerful; and gentle, delicate efforts:
sudden, rapid; and leisured, sustained efforts:
direct, penetrating; and flexible, circuitous efforts:
free, abandoned; and restrained, controlled efforts.

Combinations and shadings of these are always in evidence whenever movement occurs. To discuss them we have to answer the questions "How does the movement occur? With what quality?"

3. SPACE: WHERE THE BODY MOVES

Whenever the body moves it is displaced in space. It moves somewhere. It may move away from or back towards its own centre; or around its own centre; it may lift away from the ground or sink nearer to the ground; it may cross its own centre line or spread away from it; it may reach forwards into the space ahead or retreat backwards into itself; it may tip and lean away from its base. As these spatial displacements take place, the parts of the body trace patterns in the air that create transitory forms and structures like moving architecture. By attending to this aspect of movement we answer the question "Where does the movement go?"

4. RELATIONSHIP

The relationship of the physical nature of the body with its psychic energies and its existence in space is our concern. We are concerned with the relationship of one part of the body to another part and to the whole body; we are concerned with the relationship of one effort to another; we are concerned with the relationship of one trace form to another. We are also concerned with the relationship of the moving person with his environment and with other moving persons.

None of these four aspects, of course, exists in isolation. Human movement cannot happen without the human body; it does not exist unless effort is present; it must occur in space; as soon as it appears it has relationship to itself, the environment and other people. In the next three chapters work will be selected from the effort, space, and relationship aspects of movement in the human body, but an attempt will be made to keep in sight the essential integration of these facets of movement. They have been separately considered here only for the purposes of study, after which they are not again isolated until the last chapter, which studies their relevance within the framework of actual teaching experience.

CHAPTER 2

Dynamics

TOUGH, rugged and strenuous activities are usually regarded as essential ingredients of work in physical education with men and boys. When boys crawl out of a session, bathed in perspiration, then the point is conceded by most men that the session has been a good one. On the whole, people think that strong, powerful action is manly, and, in view of this prevailing attitude in our society, it seems sensible and strategic to use situations in which strenuous activity is involved as a starting point for any new work in movement with boys. We have found that one of the first stages in gaining interest in and respect for dance has been the recognition that it can be physically demanding. A range of energetic movement is explored in a variety of situations in this chapter, in order to suggest some ways of enlisting the masculine potential for strength in expressive movement. We wish to stress, however, that we do not subscribe to the view that only powerful action is masculine: we simply make use of this attitude in order to begin to extend the range of possibilities in boys' work.

Activities

Activities such as jumping and rolling require a considerable amount of energy, and if they are repeated time after time some very strenuous movement results. It is important, however, in the repeated performance of bodily actions in dance, that the expressive content of the movement should be aroused as well as the will and determination to persist with the performance. This is one of the most important differences between dance-like phrases of movement, and movements which are repeated and perfected for athletic or industrial purposes. In both expressive and functional movement it is important to draw out the effort content, the dynamic quality with which the movement is executed. But whereas in athletic and industrial operations the effort quality serves the purpose of the movement (*e.g.* clearing the bar or tightening the screw), in dance the effort is at the heart of the expression of the movement and is stressed for its own sake. And just as the purpose of various activities differs so does the expression of activities differ: the inherent expression of, say, jumping is different from the expression of rolling. The expressive nature of the movement will be stirred and clarified if, during the repetition of the phrases, words are used to coax the feeling of the movement—words like "jab" and "stab" are more expressive than "hop" in *e.g.* (1) below.

The following four activities require the application of long or short periods of strong exertion which are either directly focused or more sinuous.

ACTIVITY 1

Starting position: upright with the right foot slightly in front of the left. Hop on alternate feet—hop right—hop left—hop right—hop left—hop right—hop left, in a swift sequence of six hops. Jab into the air.

In a hopping jump, the same foot that drives the body from the ground also receives the body weight first in the landing. Thrust away from the ground with the take-off foot. Make these hops increase in size from very small to very large.

Increase the explosive quality of the jump by using the other knee to help in the upward drive. Make your knees stab upwards.

Bunch the body into a compact shape and make it penetrate upwards into the air like a rocket. Try to get a swifter punch from your feet and legs: touch down after each hop only in order to project yourself into the air again. Grip in the whole body as you drive it into the air.

ACTIVITY 2

Starting position: upright with feet astride. Jump around, through 180°, so that you are suddenly facing the opposite direction. Repeat, in reverse, so that you return to your starting position. Whip around in a clockwise direction so that your right side initiates and leads the turn: whip around in an anti-clockwise direction so that your left side initiates and leads the turn.

One moment you face the teacher and the next moment you have your back to him. There is an element of surprise present. Use your arms to lash around the body—round and back—round and back. Your arms should swing powerfully through the air.

If you use the whole of your right side, including your leg, to initiate this slash you will be able to turn completely round through 360°. In preparation, gather your right side across the body, support your weight on the left foot only, and now lash around in a complete turn.

Gather the left side in preparation, with the right foot supporting the body weight, and whip around in an anti-clockwise direction. Use both legs actively in the air and do not let them simply hang.

These jumping turns can be performed twice in quick succession and they should have the quality of a powerful whip-lash.

Both (1) and (2) require sudden bursts of strength. In (1) the sudden strength is exerted in a compact, penetrating manner and in (2) the sudden strength is exerted everywhere around, diversely. The next two activities require strength of a more enduring and persistent kind.

ACTIVITY 3

Starting position: upright, with the right foot placed in front of the left, and the body evenly carried on both feet. Exert firm pressure downwards until both knees are bent and the body is supported on the right foot and the left knee. Press into the ground and raise the body with the same slow strong exertion, and place the left foot forward so that the sinking and lifting can be repeated on the other foot and knee before release of tension. There must be no slackening of muscular tension until the body has been lowered and raised twice. Maintain an evenly firm pressure throughout. Out-turn the feet and knees as the body drives downwards and use the weight of the body to intensify the strength of the downward pressure. Attention should be focused on the straight pathway marked by the front knee. There should be a relentless power in the persistent performance of this slow press.

ACTIVITY 4

Starting position: sitting cross-legged on the floor. Keep the lower half of the body firmly planted on the floor as you strongly wind the left side of the body, led by the left elbow, across the right side of the body to touch the floor. As the body is tipped onto its side, the same slow grinding power will writhe the hips and legs over and over, so that firm twisting, winding rolls along the floor are produced. These, of course, will be performed in rhythmic, repetitive phrases set by the teacher (wind over and over and over), or determined by the individual boy. In the first instance rhythmic phrasing is achieved by the simple repetition of action and recovery—the movement being performed two, three, four, five or so times—and then repeated the *same* number of times. When rhythmical flow is established a stress in a phrase usually becomes apparent, *e.g.* the jumps get bigger as the phrase concludes or the turning begins more quickly than it finishes.

These energetic activities involving strong muscular tension call upon certain sources of human potential, leaving others untapped. They in fact illustrate four of the eight basic effort actions.*

When boys are given sequences that consist entirely of such actions they cannot maintain them for very long. Either the dynamic quality of the sequences degenerates into a feeble mechanical performance, or some sort of recovery period begins to appear within the phrase. Perhaps there is a release of tension after each jump in (1), or during the turn in (2), or as the body moves through the starting position during the repetition of (3) and (4). In order to keep going, the boys have to have a breather or have to establish a rhythmic interplay of exertion and recovery. A similar need is seen very clearly in skilled working actions and in some games activities. It is also needed in dance.

Experiences that would provide compensation for the energetic activities described would have a certain fineness and delicacy—a quality which, of course, is as much within the range of a man as a woman—but a quality which has been neglected or left haphazardly to chance in men's physical education. Any educational experience that purports to explore and develop full human potential must take both firm and gentle qualities of movement into account.

Activities Further Developed

The four activities already described could be developed in the following ways in order to make rhythmical and balanced sequences.

* Laban & Lawrence, *Effort* (Macdonald & Evans); Laban, *Modern Educational Dance* (Macdonald & Evans); Laban, *Mastery of Movement* (Macdonald & Evans).

DEVELOPMENT 1

The firm, thrusting hops can be repeated time and time again very vigorously if, at the end of each phrase of, say, six hops, a slow turn around is completed whilst a deep breath is taken. Then the sequence is repeated with its re-charging jabbing, stabbing quality. Allow the sustained turn to rise and spread slightly as the minimum amount of muscular tension is used during this easy floating turn.

DEVELOPMENT 2

The slashing turning jumps to right and left can be executed repeatedly if three smooth, even steps forward are taken after each pair of jumps. The whipping, lashing quality is compensated for and re-charged by the light steady gliding steps that proceed directly forward.

DEVELOPMENT 3

The firm sustained application of pressure in raising and lowering the body can be repeated with continued quality if a small releasing, light jump is made after each sequence of two deep steps. Shake the body lightly in the air during this jump, so that the movement has a quick, flickering quality in contrast to the even directed pressure of the main action.

DEVELOPMENT 4

The twisting spiralling downwards and upwards will be more effectively maintained if the strong tension is released into a series of four quick light steps that dart forward before the wringing downwards re-commences in a new place in the room. The four steps should be dab-like, delicate, over in a flash as they carry the body straight to the new spot.

From the beginning, we suggest that the main energetic action should be stressed with boys. When they begin to tire, the stress should be switched to the compensatory action and, gradually, this should be improved to the same qualitative standard as the firm, strong movement; although, quantitatively, there will be less of it in the overall sequence.

These examples pin-point one of the important differences between dance phrases and, say, gymnastic skills. The release and recovery necessary in the latter for an effective performance is judged by the performance: in dance phrases, the "compensation" is in itself as expressive and positive as the main action: it exists in its own right: it is different in quality and is not merely a release. The recovery is part of the organic structure of the dance phrase. The phrases given can be mastered individually by boys, and also be performed in twos, when the boys then have to arrange themselves in relation to their partners and bring out the movement expression of the phrase in relation to their partner. For example, (1) can be performed by two boys facing each other, several yards apart, and with an attitude of readiness. The thrusting jumps take them past each other's right shoulder until they arrive in the starting position originally held by their partner. The gentle, floating turns then enable them to face their partners again. Possibly the advancing jumps would show increasing belligerence, which is then frustrated in the passing and finally resigned in the turning.

All activities can be classified into forms of *travelling* (creeping, sliding, rolling, running): forms of *jumping* (hopping, bouncing, bounding, taking off from one foot and arriving on two, taking off from two feet and arriving on one): forms of *turning* (pivoting on the right foot while the left leg swings the body round anti-clockwise in an open turn, or the left leg swings the body round clockwise in a closed turn): forms of *gesture* in which there is no concern for transference of weight (sinking, writhing, or spreading the body on the spot). Any of these actions can be used in sequences, and the dynamics of the sequences built into expressive phrases by the teacher and/or the class. At the end of this chapter is a description of a lesson, based on action phrases, that was taken with 14-year-old boys who had never danced before in their secondary school P.E. programme.

Dance Drama

Dance drama has provided many people with a successful way of arousing the effort participation of boys who were being introduced to expressive movement.*

Here, again, we suggest that the initial emphasis might be on the energetic and strenuous, and so situations of conflict or power or aggression could be chosen to capture the interest of the boys. Battles, marching armies, warring

* Garard & Wiles, *Leap to Life;* Russell, *Modern Dance in Education* (Macdonald & Evans); Bruce, *Lord of the Dance* (Pergamon Press).

groups, hunting and fighting give full play to the actions of thrusting and slashing and pressing and wringing, which we explored in the first part of this chapter within activities of the body that appeal to boys. The narratives which usually provide the framework for such dance dramas usually also provide the compensatory experiences of movement—the comic relief, the care for the injured, the protection of the vulnerable, etc. During the battles and wars actions of powerful effort are used and then, during the questing or safeguarding or resting, the more delicate, gentle qualities.

Dance drama, however, if it is not to be a degenerate form of mime, usually needs more experience to handle than the inexperienced teacher recognises. We have found that general, rather than specific, *dramatic situations* can be handled very effectively by the newcomer to expressive movement. We are confining our suggestions to the situations we have used with secondary school boys. (See also Plates 1–3)

SITUATION I

Starting position: alone and near the ground with eyes fixed on the floor. When you hear the drum roll in the distance—look into the distance as if searching for the sound. The sound will grow and fly overhead, then recede into the distance. Follow the sound with your eyes as though tracking it. Next time, when overhead, the sound will explode. What do you do? Throw yourself on the ground? Cower away? Remain fixed in stunned immobility? Break into panic? Repeat this several times and clarify the changes in muscular tension in the body. Is there a build-up or a slackening of tension? Is there a flurry of movement or a freezing? Try this in groups of four or five boys. The "thing" passes overhead the first time and only explodes the second time. Work as a group, and decide what you will do as a result of the explosion.

SITUATION 2

Starting position: in threes in a triangular formation with one boy leading. A journey begins, with the trio staying close together and crawling or darting or dashing to a new part of the room. These ways of travelling may be tried individually during the first part of the lesson. Each boy takes over the leadership in turns, to make a three-part journey which grows in

20

excitement as the "object" of the search is tracked down. Try this again, ensuring that each leader takes the journey one stage nearer the end of the search; let them learn the floor track—does it curve or zig-zag, or go straight ahead? How is each part of the journey made? Is it cautious, confident, excited, tentative? Does each boy, eventually, after he has had time to improvise, repeat his part of the journey accurately? When the boys get to the end of the journey they surround the "object" and do something with it to show what they were tracking. Do they stamp on it, screw it up, stroke it, pick it up carefully, kick it or eat it? (Plates 4–7 show one reaction)

SITUATION 3

Starting position: alone in a space "guarding treasure from attack." They show, in the way they move around this treasure that it is fragile, vulnerable and valuable. Care and protection are interspersed with anxious glances around. Anxiety increases until complete attention has to be focused on an attack from outside. Build this phrase from stillness, into concern for the treasure, into anxiety and into a fight with an imaginary opponent for the safety of the treasure. Finally, at the end of the struggle show that the outcome is of a triumphant or dispirited nature. This could be taken in small groups, also, which then could build up the following:

(a) *"A protecting" motif* around the treasure. This could be a step worked out and performed in unison, and expressing care and concern.

(b) *A series of sorties* by different individuals who take it in turn to reconnoitre. Each must work out a travelling step pattern and repeat this on each occasion he leaves the group. These reconnoitrings will carry an expression of anxiety and searching.

(c) *The preparations to defend the treasure* as danger appears, followed by the fight.

(d) *The rejoicing dance of victory* (Plate 8) or the defeated withdrawal of the vanquished.

Such episodes embody recurring myths about the dilemma of the human race, and each boy or group of boys could, if desired, give each episode a specific, personal context. It is very important that these dramatic situations are formed and repeated and clarified, and not left as mere improvisations which provide little satisfaction for older boys. Suggestions about coaching are contained in Chapter 5. An illustration of a lesson taken with 14-year-old boys is given at the end of this chapter.

Music

ADVANTAGES; SELECTION AND USE

Possibly one of the most direct methods of arousing the effort participation of boys is to use *music* with a dynamic stress. This has an immediate appeal, and places the firm sudden or firm sustained accents within the framework of rhythmic phrases. In the early stages of introducing dance, it is important to choose short pieces of music or short extracts from longer works in order that a reasonable standard of movement mastery is achieved. Repetition within pieces is also very useful and helps to consolidate movement expression. It is our experience that boys find most satisfaction from skilful mastery of movement in this way, rather than from the prolonged improvisation demanded by a lengthy piece of music. They are enabled to discover the inherent meaning of movement, by searching for and formulating clear expression in a way that eludes them when movement remains at the constantly improvisatory level.

Lists of music on record or tape that have been found useful for dance are given in *Modern Dance in Education* by Russell, *Leap to Life* by Garard & Wiles, and *Lord of the Dance* by Bruce. Several of the bands from the "Listen and Move" records published by Macdonald & Evans are also appropriate for this age group. The following list consists of music we have used specifically with boys during the last two years:

A Jumping Game—Shishov.   H.M.V.
A Joke—Kabilevsky.   H.M.V.
Alexander Nevsky—Prokoviev.   R.C.A. Victor.
Beatle Cracker Suite.   H.M.V. 7EG 8919.
Carmen Suite—Bizet.   Fidelio ATL 4036.
Carmina Burana—Orff.
Concert of English Music.   ACL 113.
Dances—Mozart and Haydn.   K.586.   T.V. 4011.
Four Studies for Small Orchestra—Sravinsky.   Decca CEP 5509.

Heroic Music for Brass and Percussion—played by E. Power Biggs. C.B.S. BRG 72077.

Hungarian Dances—Brahms.   Concert Hall M. 942.

Les Patineurs—Meyerbeer.   ADD. 139.

Music for Trumpet and Orchestra.   ACL R56.

Music in Spanish American Style.   Capitol LCT 6141.

Sergeant Pepper's Lonely Hearts Club Band.

Spanish Gypsy Dance.   Pye 7N 15485.

Six Interlinked Dances—Mozart.   K.509.   Decca BR 3082.

The Marionettes—Rosenberg.   Decca.

Three Austrian Dances—Mozart.   K.V. 606.

We also use a great deal of popular music, but as this is so rapidly outdated it is not included on this list.

Music can be selected because of its value as a stimulus to expressive movement. If music is to be used in this way in a lesson, then the lesson could begin with a general warming up to enliven the kinaesthetic responses of the class. After this warming up but before the music is played, the boys need to be grouped in threes or fives, or whatever number they are working with, or they need to remain quietly alone. Then when the music is played the class will be encouraged to improvise. With boys in the primary age range and with older boys who are used to working creatively in school it is not difficult. For boys whose education has been more rigid, it is a virtually impossible approach and one which the teacher would do well to avoid in favour of a more directed starting point. The improvisations should be repeated several times in order that the boys can find their own response in movement. After this stage verbal questions asked by the teacher and answered in movement by the class will help the boys to clarify their movement:

Is this firm energy contrasted anywhere by delicate energy? Do the firmness and the gentleness appear in sudden flashes or in a slow, steady manner?

Is the strength in your sequence of a wringing or whipping kind that is everywhere around, or is it of a pressing or punching kind that is channelled in its focus?

Is the gentleness of a flickering or floating kind, or is it a directed dabbing or gliding?

Such questions can be asked generally in the class, but a great deal of individual help will also have to be given in this sort of situation. There is, of course, a world of difference between the challenge of producing an individual and meaningful movement sequence and the self-indulgence of "do as you please."

On the other hand, a piece of music can be selected because it seems to the teacher to support specific ideas of movement that the teacher wishes to use with the class in a structured way. In this case, the teacher would devise the movement sequences for the class to master. We have used for example the first part of Mozart's *Six German Dances* to give an experience of changes of effort with secondary school boys. The first phrase is repeated three times.

Phrase 1. This was used to stimulate and accompany four explosive leaps that shot into the air, before a gentle turning on the spot and a quick travelling to a new place in the room. A thrusting, punching quality was brought out in the leaps (eliciting the firmness, suddenness, directness): a floating in the turning (eliciting the gentleness, the sustainment, the flexibility): a darting in the travelling (eliciting the light, swift, direct steps). Thus confident leaps gave way to a rather hesitant turn, and then to quick decisive steps.

After practising this sequence individually the boys grouped in fours, but then took up their starting positions away from the group. By the end of the first phrase the group of four boys had arrived in a small circle of four.

Phrase 2. Each boy, in turn, introduced himself, so to speak, by leaping into the air once (instead of four times as in phrase 1). Then the group turned in unison and darted round its own circle in a clockwise direction, consolidating itself round a central focus.

Phrase 3. As phrase 2 but with the unison turning and darting in an anti-clockwise direction.

Phrase 4. A welding of the group in the explosive jumping part, followed by individual turning away from the group and darting back to each boy's original starting position.

PLATES 1–3

A rhythmicised sequence worked at individually. From a starting position near the ground, attention was focused high, then a journey made towards this high focus. During the journey it was important to bring out the attitude of the boy towards his journey—delight, apprehension, wonder and so on. In Plate 3 (*inset, below*) the goal has been achieved and a short dance sequence results.

PLATES 4–7

Rhythmic group sequence. The leap had to be synchronised in order to finish together. No verbalising was permitted—the group had to feel when to strike in unison. Some degree of group empathy had to be built up before even partial success was possible, but once this had been achieved a great deal of satisfaction resulted from this synchronised timing. Each person's strike had to be exactly repeated and in time a group rhythm was established, resulting in exciting group shapes such as those illustrated.

PLATE 6
The kill. Note the concentration of focus of the group and the hands attending to the detail of what is being carried as a weapon.

PLATE 7
A group catching the object of their choice. Note details of hands and focus of heads and eyes.

PLATE 8

A trio working in unison on a triumphal dance. This utilised the five basic jumps in an exuberant finale to sequences devised by the boys. They worked individually and then came together in this single formation.

It need hardly be said that this is one of very many possible uses of this particular music. The group could start together and gradually, one at a time, boys could leave the group and then return to it. The music could be used by two boys or by two groups to work out a question-and-answer dance.

Both these methods—the one in which the class improvises and is helped by the teacher to clarify, and the other in which the dance happenings are formulated by the teacher and taught directly to the boys—have a place in expressive movement work. Sometimes a compromise between the two methods is the best way of initiating movement inventiveness in older boys, to whom the activity of creating in movement is alien at first. In such a compromise, the teacher would work out the framework of the dance sequence, so that the boys were required to contribute at certain places within the framework. Using the same Mozart music it is possible to evolve such a framework. We would coach the four thrusting jumps at the beginning of each phrase, and leave the remainder of each phrase as a recovery and preparation period. Then the boys would be encouraged to improvise during the remainder of each phrase, and find a satisfactory balance or resolution to the thrusting jumps. This they could do alone or in small groups as they chose. As well as the four thrusting jumps, it might be advisable to stipulate that the jumping is to begin alone, but by the end of the third phrase the boys must have come into relationship in twos, threes or fours ready to perform the final phrase in unison. Here again the parts contributed by the boys need to be clarified by questions from the teacher, so that a mastered and coherent expression results, and not a woolly, indeterminate improvisation. Using this method of part-teacher/part-boys a confidence is given to older boys—but it must be admitted that inventiveness rather than creativeness results.

SELF-CREATED MUSIC

Far the best for beginners is popular music. Its contemporary flavour removes some of the suspicion from an unfamiliar activity. The repetition and the undemanding nature of popular music means that every boy's concentration can be devoted to the experience of movement. Ultimately, the perpetual use of music places severe restrictions on the movement experiences derived by any class, but in the initial stages and, indeed, periodically afterwards, music is a very valuable stimulus and accompaniment. The qualitative, dynamic aspects of dance have much in common with the dynamic nuances of music. And the phrasing of the music assists the planning of the dance in its flow of action and recovery. Musical climaxes also promote climaxes and stresses in mood and structure of the movement.

Percussion instruments provide a useful stimulus for dynamic action. They are comparatively simple to handle, yet give beginners a sense of security in providing them with a tangible object to hold. Weight changes (between firm and gentle) are readily produced by soft and loud sounds, and time changes (sudden and sustained) can be played. Short compositions in sound can be created by individuals or small groups of boys using similar or different instruments and then a composition in movement can be made to accompany this. Alternatively a movement sequence made by the boys can be accompanied by percussion invented by another group of boys. But most rewarding and satisfying is the creation of a dance sequence along with a percussion composition. We have found older boys very interested in this dual activity even in the early introductory stages. Not all secondary schools, however, have access to a wide range of percussion instruments, and so the illustration of percussion work at the end of this chapter is one in which parts of the body are used percussively in clapping and stamping. It is not suggested, however, that body percussion is merely a substitute for instruments. Boys enjoy the experience of making their own sounds to accompany dance, and, what is more, an improvement in the quality of movement often results from this direct relationship between sound and movement.

Specific Dance Sessions with Boys

The most valuable imaginative and dramatic themes for dance will arise from the current interests and preoccupations of particular classes and their teachers. Though some suggestions for themes which might lend themselves to this level of personal exploration will be made in various places in the book, no details of possible developments nor descriptions of lessons based on them will be included. This is to avoid the danger of imposing a stereotype of experiences which should be particular to the group concerned.

Instead, the lessons described involve material of a more general nature which could be enjoyed by a wide range of pupils.

I. ACTION WORDS

In this session action words were used to stimulate expressive movement. The words were chosen because they gave an action to perform (jump, turn, step, sink, stop), plus a clear indication of how to perform this action, *e.g.* whirl=turn quickly: creep=step cautiously. Each word had *Action+Effort*, and was consequently more evocative than action words alone, such as run, jump, bend, stretch. (See Plates 9–11.)

During the first half of the session the teacher guided the boys through movement phrases built from expressive words, and tried to reach the expression of movement through the coaching of these phrases. In the second half of the session the boys were given the opportunity to select their own phrases and also to work in small groups.

(a) *The warm-up.* This was based on shaking and gripping, which was taken first in the hands, where the looseness of the wrists and fingers in the shaking was contrasted with the firm, held grip. It is important to tell the boys to look at their hands in order to focus attention. The shaking was taken into the arms and shoulder girdle along with the hands, and the gripping also was extended into the arms and shoulders. Finally the shaking and gripping were taken into the spine and hips, so that the participation of the whole body was enlisted. Each of these stages was repeated in a phrase, and then all three stages were linked to give a phrase that grew in size as more and more of the body was involved.

(b) *"Toss and freeze."* Facing a partner, the boys used a tossing movement of the whole body to lift themselves into the air so that they threw themselves towards the ceiling. The phrase "toss and toss and freeze, as you focus on your partner" was worked on, so that the toss developed a certain energetic violence, while the freeze was still and poised. Attention had to be drawn to the use of the legs to drive the body into the air, and the need to "re-charge" during the freeze in order that the tossing did not lose its vitality. Practising this became rather tiring, and the quality of the movement began to be lost, so it was suggested that the boys alternated their phrases. Boy A tossed and tossed and froze and, as he came into stillness, B tossed and tossed and

27

froze. The stillness became both a recovery from the tossing and a preparation for the tossing. The sensitive alternation of A and B had to be coached. "Watch your partner while you are still, in order that you can leave the ground immediately he freezes into stillness."

(c) "*Creep and pause.*" From the still situation facing a partner, each boy crept away and then paused to look back at his partner. The teacher accompanied this verbally "creeping steadily, silently to a new spot, pausing to look around, then creeping steadily—etc." to give a rhythmic phrase. This was repeated several times in exactly the same way, and then the teacher said, "Keep the same length of creeping and the same length of pause each time—and keep going without me."

During (c) there was a hushed atmosphere after the excitement of (b). The use of the feet in careful placing and the smooth transference of weight were coached in the creeping. There was a tendency to maintain the body carriage with a tension in the shoulder and hands and back during the creeping, and so this was then stressed by the teacher as a contrast to the twist of the trunk during the looking around when the feet were still.

(d) "*Whirl and anchor.*" The situation the boys arrived in at the end of the creeping was held and the teacher said, "Now whirl and whizz around on the spot as you look around the whole room—now grip the floor with your feet as you anchor yourself quite still." The phrase of whirling and anchoring was repeated and the dizzy, intoxicating whirling was contrasted with the safe, widely-based stillness.

(e) "*Slither and melt.*" The boys were asked to let the stillness melt onto the floor. This odd expression was effective in producing expressive movement and then the boys slithered away before transferring their weight back onto their feet and darting back to their starting position. Melt, slither, dart were repeated. The systematic collapsing of the body part by part—knees, seats, shoulders, in the melting—was then transformed into the lithe, sinuous twisting and writhing of the slithering and then into the quick, short, light, darting steps.

It was obvious during this phrase that some boys were imagining themselves in dramatic situations (*e.g.* "being shot," "slithering through undergrowth"). The teacher was quite happy for this to happen, but did not force it or comment on it on this occasion, because these personal fantasies

28

varied, and it was equally obvious that other boys were simply absorbed in the movement for its own sake and would have been distracted by such comments. The teacher, instead, concentrated on the quality and the expressiveness of the movement, and his remarks were focused on giving bodily help (*e.g.* "at the end of the slithering get yourself into such a position that you can step forward—get your weight over your feet"), in order to intensify the effort quality (*e.g.* "in the melting there is a smooth giving in to the weight of the body; in the slithering there is a flexible deviousness; in the darting there is a quick burst of speed"). On another occasion he might have assisted by drawing out and helping to make explicit the dramatic elements

(f) *Blackboard work.* At this point the class was taken round a blackboard on which five lists of words were written.

toss	creep	whirl	shake	pause
explode	slither	swivel	wobble	freeze
soar	dart	whip	vibrate	anchor

The attention of the boys was drawn to the fact that they had already experienced something from each column. Could they understand the categories used? They quickly reached the conclusion that:

column 1 listed methods of jumping,
column 2 listed methods of travelling,
column 3 listed methods of turning, and
column 5 listed methods of being still.

Column 4 was more puzzling, and they needed help to see that these movements happened in the body without transference of weight from the spot.

Additions to these columns were invited and the following were suggested —shoot, whizz, wheel, shudder and perch.

All this section (f) took no more than five minutes to complete and we think it is important to stress this.

(g) *Sequence work.* The boys were asked to select three words (each from different columns) and make a sequence of these in any order. At this point the teacher moved around the class helping individuals.

(h) *Group sequences.* The boys were grouped in fives and, together, performed short phrases of shaking and gripping, whizzing and holding, bouncing and perching. The teacher concentrated his coaching on the relationship of the boys, and encouraged them to watch each other and work together until a common rhythm emerged. The boys were advised not to talk but to keep moving, to watch, to listen, and to adjust to each other as the group moved.

Finally each group chose its own words from the blackboard to stimulate a group sequence. Some of these were performed in unison throughout, but most groups chose to move individually or in twos as well as in unison. As these lessons were invariably taken in gymnasia, the boys often used the wall-bars in their sequences—they bounded from them into a slithering group, or crept alongside them before darting across the room.

On another occasion, the teacher distributed lists of words on cards to trios of boys who then worked on the given phrases. The boys can be asked to contribute words to future sessions.

2. SYMBOLIC FIGHTS

This was an experience in which a fight was symbolised without any blows actually making contact. It provided a range of experiences of movement, and could be used in a variety of dramatic situations devised by the boys. Similarly, fencing or fighting with sticks and swords could be symbolised in this way. (See Plates 14–16.)

(a) *Shadow boxing.* The session began with the boys facing the teacher and standing ready to fight—with the weight on the balls of the feet and fists protecting the head. Bouts of shadow boxing provided an introductory activity, with the feet moving quickly on the floor and then pausing in alert stillness in preparation for the next bout. This was repeated several times, with the teacher highlighting the difference between the sudden light dabbing feet and the sudden stinging punches of the fists. "Rat-at-at-at-at-at-at" phrase.

(b) *Hit and fall.* The teacher then said to the class that he was going to pretend to hit them on the chin and knock them onto the floor. They took up a crouching, defensive position and the teacher drove a blow towards the class, accompanying it with a "woomph" sound. The boys stayed still on the floor after being knocked down, and it was pointed out that this was a different bodily situation from the starting position. This was repeated several times—some boys crumpling under the blow, others keeling over backwards or sideways. The attention of the boys was drawn to the fact that the blow hit the chin first, and so this had to be shown clearly in each boy's response.

(c) *Hit and recover*. Three blows were delivered in succession so that each boy had to recover and return to his feet without any pause on the ground. The phrase then became: hit-fall and recover-hit-fall and recover-hit-fall and recover. It was pointed out that although no blow actually reduced them to stillness on the floor as in (b), each blow affected them so that when they had recovered and were back on their feet, there was something different from their original starting position, *e.g.* maybe their guard had dropped on one side, or both fists were carried lower, or the head was lifted and turned. They were encouraged to show the result of the blows in this way. The phrase of three blows was repeated several times.

(d) *Hit and spin*. The teacher explained that he would now hit them on the right shoulder so that they were spun around by the impact. It was repeated on the left shoulder also, and the resulting body carriage was again different.

(e) *Hit and double up*. The teacher then hit them in the stomach so that they doubled up forwards as they dropped onto the ground, and some rolled over. Again, this was repeated in a phrase.

(f) *Multiple blows*. The blow on the chin was followed by the blow on one shoulder and the blow in the stomach. The boys were asked to emphasise clearly the body part that received the blow, and the result of the blow through their carriage. Up to this point the teacher had accompanied each blow with a vocal sound and/or the sound of his fist striking his other palm, but now he used a tambour. A loud bang indicated each blow and a softer drum roll indicated the reaction and recovery period. This stimulated the rhythmic flow of the phrase.

(g) *Partner work*. In twos, each pair of boys worked out a fighting sequence using some of the "blows" practised plus others that they devised—kicking away of legs, kneeing in the stomach, double-handed chops at the neck, etc. Exciting and expressive phrases were built up (as in Plates 14–16).

(h) *The teacher circulates around the class*. At this stage the teacher helps pairs to clarify their sequences by circulating around the class. He made the general point to the class that the striker must follow through his blow, as well as giving each blow a clear start, *e.g.* a blow from the floor that soared upwards past the jaw and into the air: or one that started across the body and whipped past his opponent's face to finish wide on the open side of the body.

We have always found this sequence a very popular one with older boys, and have usually followed it up by setting the class a problem. This has been to devise a situation that culminates in the fight sequence they have already worked out, or to make the fight the starting situation and allow some other event to arise from it. Because the fight has been symbolised and patterned into a rhythmic structure it emerges as dramatic dance and not as a stage fight.

3. CLAPPING AND STAMPING

In this session the sounds produced by clapping hands, stamping feet and vocal "zzzz-zzzz" sounds were used to stimulate dance phrases in which effort changes were used.

(a) *Clapping with the teacher*. The teacher faced the class and clapped a rhythm. This was clapped alternately by the class and the teacher, and participation by the whole body in the clapping was encouraged even though the body was comparatively still.

(b) *Clapping and dancing by class and teacher*. As the class clapped, the teacher danced; as the teacher clapped, the class danced. They were encouraged to keep the rhythm but make this clear in the whole body in action—in whirling and flying and beating and hopping, rather than in the hands alone.

(c) *Clapping and dancing in twos*. The partner relationship between the class and the teacher was then changed to a partner relationship in twos in which one boy clapped, the other danced and vice-versa. The teacher stressed that *both* boys were involved all the time.

(d) *Jumping*. The dancing was then restricted to jumping only, and for a time the class worked on this with the teacher. He first encouraged a variety of jumps to the rhythm he clapped, and then he varied the sound of the clapping. The boys explored a variety of jumps and performed them energetically when the teacher clapped loudly, and lightly when he clapped softly. Similarly, the boys were restricted to stepping and turning,

PLATE 9

Plates 9–11 show responses to action-words. In this case the two boys are using the word "wobble."

PLATE 10

"The approach." An expressive sequence showing extreme concentration: "You must not be seen or heard—you must be aware of the object you are approaching at all times." Note the effect, in the hands and feet—delicacy of placement and sustained control.

PLATE 11

"Swooping." The facial expressions show the effort and control required to produce the change of level at speed.

PLATES 12 and 13
A sequence based on the words "creep and dive." Notice the total commitment of the boys: some seem to revel in the actions themselves and enjoy, for instance, the daring of the dive; others seem to show involvement in a dramatic episode and are concerned with being a character in a specific situation.

PLATES 14 and 15
In Plates 14–15, the boys are working individually on a fight sequence, responding to blows. Some show clearly, by the way in which they stagger or spin or rebound, the part of the body—chin or shoulder or stomach—that has received the punch: others simply fall or lower themselves to the ground.

PLATE 16
The fight sequence developed in pairs. The wary, compact anticipation of one boy is in strong contrast
to the more violent reeling reaction of the other.

and these activities were experienced with firmness and with delicacy within the framework of the original rhythmic phrase.

(e) *Repeating phrases.* The boys returned to work in twos and tried to produce variations of effort within their phrases. They each consolidated a phrase that they could repeat, which contained an interplay of firm, delicate, sudden and sustained movements.

(f) *Phrases with "zzzz" sounds.* Still in twos, facing partners, the boys produced "zzzz" sounds through their teeth as they sank onto their knees in unison, and then lifted themselves high into the air to this continuous, steady sound. There were no breaks or sharp changes as in the clapping.

The boys kept the "zzzz" sound and made a phrase in which they stayed together the whole time—stepping, circling, spreading, etc. Attention was placed on remaining with one's partner and keeping the movement continuous.

(g) *The final dance.* This consisted of the original clapping phrase performed alternately by each boy, followed by the continuous "zzzz" section, in which the couple moved together, and finally there was a repeat of the clapping section.

The transitions between the parts will always be poor with beginners. We suggest that stillness is stressed when the clapping section is completed, and then—with eyes fixed on each other—the two boys move slowly into their starting positions for the continuously smooth section and then begin the "zzzz" noise. There will be a similar transition from this central section to the repeat of the rhythmic section.

The suggestions for dance made in this chapter have all been chosen to give opportunities for strenuous activity. At the same time the rich range of quality embodied in the eight basic effort actions has been explored in order to provide balance. Thus the potential for delicate, sustained and flexible movement has been realised as well as for strong, sudden and direct movement. At the dramatic level the emotional qualities of protectiveness and sensitivity have been tapped as well as those of aggressiveness and daring. The stimuli have included simple action phrases, words, percussive sounds, music and broad dramatic situations. Teachers and classes, as they gain confidence, will find that part of the excitement of dance is discovering new stimuli to movement within and outside this range.

CHAPTER 3

Form and Structure

In the last chapter, action, music, words, percussive sound and dramatic situations were used to produce patterns of movement from which the effort contained in the movement was elicited. These can also produce movement happenings from which spatial tensions in movement can be elicited. This would mean that questions centred around "Where does the movement go?" would be used rather than questions centred around "How does the movement occur?" For example, from the work based on words, the teacher could ask, "What sort of pattern on the floor does the slithering make?" From the work using percussive sounds, he could ask, "At the end of your partner's clapping, when you have finished your dance, are you near the ground, high in the air, or at medium level?" And, from the fight sequence, the teacher could ask, "Do the three blows with which you strike your partner move from the centre of your body, spoke-like, or do they hit across, peripherally?" Naturally, of course, if spatial questions of this kind are to be asked the build-up of the work will also have stressed spatial aspects of movement.

When the material of dance is focused on spatial experiences and when the teacher concentrates attention on spatial configurations, then there seems to be, on the part of the class, an absorption different from the absorption found in lessons based on the effort stresses within movement.

Movement in Space

All movement occurs in space: this is an inescapable fact; but the fact can be made more prominent or it can recede into the background. When the main focus is on space, the effort enhances the space and colours it: when the main focus is on effort, the spatial clarification gives form to the effort. In Chapter 2 the spatial aspects of the movement were allowed to recede, as we tried to intensify the dynamic energies of the movement, but the spatial aspects were still present. In this chapter the spatial aspects of movement are our prime concern, and we shall allow the dynamics to play a supporting rôle.

When shape and pattern and form and structure are dominant, particular and different demands are made on the dancer. Very accurate adjustments and re-adjustments of the moving body have to be made, if the trace-forms of the movement are to be clearly defined. Only when they are clearly defined are the movements meaningful experiences and lucid expressions. This work in shape and form, because it is demanding, has been found to give considerable satisfaction to older boys. They seem ready to make this requirement of their own creative efforts and derive pleasure from this particular discipline.

There is a danger in this work. Because attention is focused on pathways and trace-forms created by the body, the inexperienced teacher can allow this to be a somewhat external concern. The straightness of the line, the size of the angle can pre-occupy the mind: and only when this pre-occupation becomes absorbed into, felt, experienced as a reality in the body, does the movement become a spatial experience. Work in space can be a mere shell, a waving and poking of limbs.

To minimise this danger it is necessary that full bodily participation is enlisted from the first. An enjoyable start can be made by exploiting the boys' delight in body shape in action—in cartwheels, rolls and twisting in the air. There is also a need to develop a sense of dancing in one's own space as well as in the general space of the room. Ideas of over, under, round, through, towards, away from, and near and far should be explored in the early stages.

Spatial aspects are visual as well as kinaesthetic and this attribute can be harnessed to good effect by the teacher. Problems can be set on the blackboard or can be written on cards for individuals or groups of boys to work out. Here are some examples.

1. CHANGES OF LEVEL

A line was drawn on the board by the teacher, who explained to the boys that it showed changes of level in a moving body—a sweep down from a high level, followed by a curving undulation, and then an even steeper climb high. The boys worked on this individually and were encouraged to bring out the rhythmic flow of the whole phrase by constantly repeating it. Most boys kept the body very symmetric, starting high on the balls of the feet and reaching upwards through the whole body, with the hand high in the air and the body carried evenly. They then travelled *forwards* through the pathway. Others drew the pattern in the space in front of them as they travelled *sideways*.

These differences were shown and the boys asked to enlist the plastic and three-dimensional nature of the body. It was suggested that they made a new part of the body take over each stage of the pathway. Fists and palms tended to be the leading parts during the first steep drop in the pathway, and the teacher had to insist that the steep line actually touched the floor before it began to undulate. Shoulders and knees and feet predominated in leading the curved section of the pathway, and then there was a return to hands at the end. Some elbows were used and one boy produced an amusing variation by leading the curved pathway with his seat in the air. The different body shapes produced at each stage of this air pattern were commented upon—the long, thin, elongated start and finish, as opposed to the bunched and rounded shape of the body during the undulating section of the phrase. Some boys then chose to work with partners and "interweave" these air patterns, whilst others remained alone and worked out their own patterns based on level changes.

2. FLOOR PATTERNS

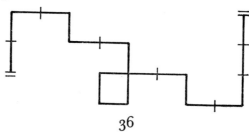

This and similar diagrams were drawn on cards and handed out to the class. The teacher explained that the diagram was of a floor pattern, an aerial view of a track, and the track was divided into steps. Each boy remained in his own area of the room and, holding his card in front of him, stepped through the floor pattern. Some boys faced the same way the whole time, *e.g.* faced the gym clock, and so some of their steps went forwards, some sideways, and some backwards: other boys faced the way they were travelling all the time and so changed their front several times although they always stepped forwards. The boys were quite intrigued when this was pointed out to them, and they were given time to try out both methods. All the diagrams on the cards used sequences of 20 steps.

As the boys practised their step patterns and tried to memorise them through doing them, the teacher began to accompany them, quietly, with a beat on a tambour. He used four bars of five beats, and repeated this time and time again, until the boys were able to dispense with their cards as they phrased their step-patterns. The teacher then coached these sequences.

"What attitude do these direction changes produce in you? Uneasy? Comic? Relentless? Bring out your attitude to these changes in your pathway."

"Make the surfaces of the body carve the pathway more clearly by determining exactly which part leads at each stage of the journey— chest, elbow, sole of the foot, etc."

"Can you emphasise the pathway more by making some steps firmer or quicker than others?"

"Keep the angles sharp as the direction changes or the body turns."

"How is the body carried—is it sometimes expansively spread or hunched up or knotted round or elongated?"

Finally, each boy chose a partner with a different floor pattern from his own, and the two boys tried to relate these two patterns by juxtaposing them in some way. Some overlapped; others were distanced. All kept to the four bars of five steps. Naturally, this could be varied.

These boys were 15-year-olds, and this proved a quite difficult task for them. At the end of the session, the teacher put on a lively rhythmic record for the boys to improvise freely to—as a release from the previous

37

concentration. Incidentally, this seemed to "free" some boys who had previously been very reluctant to improvise.

As has already been mentioned, the visual aspect of spatial work can also be a problem. The visual can become a replacement for the kinaesthetic and so cloud the real issue—the experience of movement. For instance, an angular pathway, if frozen in a diagram, becomes

The essence of its movement is the presence of two sharp changes of direction

and

and these abrupt changes immediately give it its characteristic colouring. Someone who has not been aware of angular *movement* could look at the diagram and produce merely three straight lines

which have no connection with an angular pathway.

Another problem created by diagrams is that they are essentially two-dimensional and, of course, movement of the human body is three-dimensional and plastic. With regard to this, some teachers have used mobile and abstract sculptures as effective stimuli for dance.

Some indication of the bodily demands made by simple spatial pathways is shown in the following three examples:

(a) *A circular pathway* is traced with fingers of the right hand around the body at waist height. Start with the right hand reaching across the body to the left, and with the left hand providing some counter-tension by crossing, a little, underneath the leading right arm. Keeping the feet still and slightly apart, sweep the arm clockwise around the body, passing through the furthest points of reach forwards, to the right, backwards, and finally returning to the starting position, crossed over to the left. All these situations must be passed through as near to waist level as possible, if the circle is to be accurately traced. To do this, the trunk must be moved out of the way of the encircling arm in order to aid it: the spine must be bent and twisted and stretched, the shoulders dropped, and the head must follow the line of the circle.

(b) *Angular pathways.* Step with the right foot, across the left side of the body, down to the ground, so that both knees are bent and the right hand is reaching out to the left and touching the floor. With this as the starting position, sling the hand upwards and backwards behind the head and then to the right, open side of the body and slightly forwards. If the right hand leads the movement clearly, it should trace an angular pathway that changes direction far behind the head. In this movement there is a lifting backwards of the body, as the spine stretches and untwists during a backwards step with the right foot. Then the body is opened and propelled forwards to arrive balanced on the right foot, which has stepped diagonally forwards.

(c) *A figure-of-eight-pathway* is traced, by the right hand, through a circle placed on the left side of the body followed by a circle at waist level. The first circle passes through forwards—deep—backwards—high—forwards, and is perpendicular to the ground. The second circle passes through, forwards—right—backwards—left—forwards, and is horizontal to the ground. The gathering nature of the first circle is contrasted with the scattering nature of the second circle, and produces a twist as a transition between the two circles.

As these have been described, they could provide mobilising or training sequences. Another way of utilising them is through a freer and more creative use of the trace-forms.

In example (a) the swinging, sweeping, circular movements easily lead into turning and spiralling, so that architectural structures or "cages" are formed in the space. We have used this idea in threes and the boys have intensified the "orbiting" expression through contrast with carefully placed moments of stillness.

In example (b) the penetrating, angled abruptness of the movement has been explored by boys in twos (see Plates 17 and 19). They faced each other and produced combat-type sequences, in which each boy made his angular movement begin where his partner's finished, so that an alternating cut and thrust resulted.

39

In example (c) the twisted pathways lead readily to turns, knotted-up body shapes, and changes of attention. Pairs of boys have worked out "surprise" sequences arising from this and produced comic results. (See Plate 22.)

Descriptions of Specific Dance Sessions

I. AIR AND FLOOR PATTERNS

This dance sequence arose from an attention to air and floor pattern. A popular piece of "beat" music of a staccato nature was used as an accompaniment.

(a) *Curved pathways in the air.* The teacher made an S pathway with his right fist as he stood facing the class. It started high above his head and to the right, swept above his head to the left and round past his waist, before curving round to brush the floor and finish across the body on the left at floor level. The whole body was enlisted in this performance, so that the starting position was high on the ball of the right foot, and the final position was crossed over, near the floor. The boys watched this S pathway and then joined in with the teacher, who accompanied the movement with "S-s-s-s-s— and recover." The attention of the boys had to be focused on the pathway their own fists were making, rather than the pathway the teacher's fist was making. They also had to be encouraged to swing the trunk into this S pathway, and not merely bob up and down with the trunk as the fist curved round. This required a great deal of individual help from the teacher.

(b) *Curved pathways in the air with changed direction.* The pathway was then revised, from near the ground to high in the air, and the phrase became "S-s-s-s-s—and reverse s-s-s-s." This was practised, also, with the left fist marking the curves, and the swing of the trunk was emphasised all the time. The boys did not find it easy to get the smoothly flowing, gradual change of direction.

(c) *Curved pathways on the floor.* A popular record with a marked beat in 4/4 time was put on by the teacher, and this immediately produced re-assurance in the class. The boys were asked to keep the smooth, sweeping curves against the background of the rhythm. After a few moments, the teacher said "Now place the S pathway in front and behind you, so that

PLATES 17 and 18

A piercing of space in which the attention is focused in a single direction, and the whole body is lined up to emphasise the penetrating nature of the movement. In the individual practice above, the boy in the foreground and the boy in the right background show this emphasis more clearly than does the boy in a more relaxed position in the background to the left. In Plate 18 (*right*) the boy in the centre has almost achieved the piercing movement as he splits the other pair of boys. The boy on the right is having difficulty in co-ordinating his phrasing with his partner.

PLATES 19–22

In these four illustrations enwrapping and encircling pathways are being explored.

Plate 19 (*above*) shows a sensitive interpretation of the theme. Note the way in which the curve of the arms is emphasised by the outward rotation of the hands and the way in which the angle of the head is tipped to continue the line of the spine.

Plate 20 (*right*): two boys working together; the movement would be enhanced if the boy on the right allowed his head to follow the curve of the pathway.

Plate 21 (*far right, top*): a trio working on meeting together using straight pathways.

Plate 22 (*far right, bottom*): circuitous pathways arrested in a body shape with firm control evidenced by the position of the feet.

PLATE 23

A couple working in unison on a "covering" or "hiding" motif. The movement proceeded into a ball shape—note that the knees are already beginning to bend.

PLATE 24

A question-and-answer sequence in which one partner responded to another in alternating phrases. The piercing attitude of the crawling boy is emphasised by the position of the arms and fingers and shows his solution to the encircling shape offered by his partner. Each response prompted a further response so that a continuous sequence evolved. Developing continuity proved a difficult task for some boys.

the S runs parallel with the floor." With the music still playing, the boys tried out this replacing of the pathway, and were then coached into leaning more into the curves and adjusting the spine around the shape of the S. The teacher said "Take the S shape into the room—enlarge it by stepping into it as you sweep around the curves. Use your trunk to emphasise the curves. Lean into them. Keep your attention on the pathway your fist is making— this trace-form should stand out clearly in the space."

These smooth, curving pathways were superimposed on staccato music. We have found that, initially, some boys are rather embarrassed by the combination of smooth pathways and lyrical music—whereas most girls enjoy this combination. The challenge of keeping the pathway *in spite of* the music seems to appeal to boys.

(d) *Angular pathways in the air.* The teacher stopped the music and faced the class again. He then made an angular pathway in the air, with his right fist, starting near the ground on the left of the body (where the S curve finished). The fist shot forward and upwards, in front of the nose, and then cut to the right side of the body and a little behind it. The boys joined in, performing this angular pathway, and the teacher coached them in the sudden change of direction, the break away, at the angle.

(e) *Angular pathways on the floor.* The boys were asked to make a similar angular pathway on the floor—as a track rather than an air pattern—and step around it. Producing the sharp angle without stopping the movement or rounding the angle was a problem, but one that seemed to interest the boys. Some of them drew the attention of the teacher to attempts made by other boys.

(f) *Mirror sequences.* In twos facing each other, the boys were given the task of mirroring exactly the S pathway and then the angular pathway made by each other. Synchronising the change of direction at the angle proved the most difficult movement and caused some amusement. As the boys practised this mirroring of each other's pathways, the teacher played the record, again, softly, in the background. This provided a framework that helped some boys in phrasing their pathways.

(g) *Pattern interchanges.* The teacher said, "You are now going to inter-change pathway ideas with your partner. One of you will make an air pattern: the other boy will observe this once and then immediately repeat the pattern on the floor as a floor pattern. Try to use the background music in the same way as your partner does whether he makes an angular or curved trace-form."

After a time for experiment, each boy decided on one air pattern that was his own, and different from his partner's pattern. The two boys then practised the floor patterns provided by each other's air pattern.

(h) *Simple dance sequence.* The dance sequence was now practised using four clear phrases in the music:

> first phrase: boy A performed air pattern,
> second phrase: boy B transferred this into a floor pattern,
> third phrase: boy B performed air pattern,
> fourth phrase: boy A transferred this into a floor pattern.

The teacher coached them in the alert stillness demanded of the boy not moving, while his partner completed his pathway—so that a pattern in the air became a pattern on the floor without any break of continuity. By now the sequences were beginning to have real structure, and the boys seemed to appreciate the architectural nature of their activity.

(i) *Complex dance sequence.* Finally the boys worked out an air pattern together that combined both curved and angular forms. They practised this and then transferred it into a floor pattern, which they performed together. Eight phrases of the music were then used:

> first phrase: both boys made composite air pattern,
> second phrase: both boys made composite floor pattern,
> third phrase: boy A—air pattern,
> fourth phrase: boy B—floor pattern,
> fifth phrase: boy B—air pattern,
> sixth phrase: boy A—floor pattern,
> seventh phrase: both boys—composite/air pattern,
> eighth phrase: both boys—composite/floor pattern,

With some classes we have left the final arrangement to the boys.

2. SPATIAL ACTIONS: STABILITY

This work arose from the spatial actions of lifting, sinking, crossing, spreading, advancing and retreating.

(a) *Lifting and sinking*. The teacher crouched near the ground as he said, "Take up this starting position, near the ground, with weight evenly carried on both feet, and with both hands touching the floor. Look at your hands as they lead you upwards, passing close to the body, until you are balanced high in the air on the balls of your feet. Sink and repeat."

This was practised several times with the teacher working with the class, and the teacher emphasised several points:

"Keep your hands and arms near the vertical centre line of the body so that the up/down stress is maintained."

"Lift the chest in rising and grip in your seats when sinking."

"Stream upwards and return securely to the spot near the ground."

The teacher then asked the boys to make a phrase in which the amount of rising increased from a short lift upwards, to a longer rising, and then the final ascent. He accompanied this with vocal sounds "ya-ta . . . ya-ta-a . . . ya-ta-a-a," but he could also have used words "and lift . . . and lift higher . . . and lift high into the air." Or he could have beaten on a tambour. When the phrase had been repeated several times, the class worked in sixes, with three boys facing three boys. They practised this in unison and then in opposition, when three boys started high, sank a little and returned high, sank deeper and returned high, and sank down to the ground.

(b) *Crossing and spreading*. The boys were asked to retain the high balanced position at the end or at the beginning of their phrase. In this situation, the teacher said, "Now spread your hands away from each other, so they begin to sink as they spread apart. When they are at waist level feel the pull of one side of the body against the other side. Feel the ribs and shoulders pulling apart. Ease this stretching, by allowing the sides of the body to shrink inwards towards the centre line of the body. Make a phrase of: pull, pull, pull apart—and shrink inwards." This spreading apart was then stressed on one side of the body and a step taken to that side. When the right side was stressed, the right foot stepped sideways to the right, and then, in the shrinking recovery, stepped across the body to the left. Now, both the spreading and crossing were experienced in the lower half of the body as well as in the upper half. The interplay between the expansive spreading apart and the more restricted crossing over was emphasised.

Again, the boys divided into groups of six and worked in unison, mirroring the spreading and crossing as three boys faced three others. They were asked to bring out the easy awareness of the other three boys during the spreading, and the difficulty of being aware of the other boys during the crossing. They then intensified first the spreading, and then the crossing, to produce turns—opening turns from the spreading, and closing turns from the crossing.

(c) *Advancing and retreating.* The boys remained in their groups of six, and were asked to form circles so that they were all equidistant from the centre and from each other in each circle. The teacher said, "Take one step forwards as you reach towards the centre of your circle with both hands, so that you are carrying yourselves on one foot and leaning forwards towards the members of your group. Now step sharply backwards onto your back foot, as you withdraw from the group and the centre of the circle, and pull yourself into yourself."

As the boys did this, the teacher accompanied them with "Reach forwards, taking plenty of time—and recoil quickly." The advancing was then practised over six counts, and a sharp withdrawal over one count. The group advanced over six counts, in unison, then, in turn, withdrew over one count, advanced over six counts, etc.

The boys worked at this until the advancing and retreating interplayed without any stillness. As soon as each boy had withdrawn he began to advance, so that he was ready to retreat again when his turn came. Some groups were able, eventually, to dispense with counting; others were completely lost without a count.

(d) *Combination of actions.* Finally, all six spatial actions, which had been experienced, were used more freely. The groups selected three or four spatial actions and made sequences of them—in unison, in two groups of three, in canon, etc.

3. SPATIAL ACTIONS: LABILITY

When movement is orientated in the directions illustrated in (2) above, stable quality is produced. Jumps, turns and steps that are directed primarily upwards, downwards, sideways or across, forwards or backwards have a compact, balanced nature because of the single pull. When movement is

44

orientated into diagonal directions it is affected by three simultaneous pulls, and this produces an off-balanced, tipping and daring feeling of lability.

(a) *Preparation.* The teacher beat a tambour for a phrase of three upright, compact jumps, followed by a brief pause. He coached the single directional stress, "Shoot directly upwards, not to the side or a little ahead—but straight to the ceiling, leading with the top of your head." After several phrases had been accompanied by the teacher, he stopped playing the tambour, and the boys were invited to make a slow recovery period of sinking to the ground and rolling over, before repeating the three staccato jumps upwards. Attention had to be drawn constantly to the need to focus high when jumping, and to focus on the ground when sinking, in order fully to rise and sink.

(b) *Introduction to labile movements.* The teacher then gathered the boys around and held up a pencil, with the lead pointing upwards. "This is the direction of the jumps you have performed. Now can you tip your jumps in the air, so that you are propelled into diagonal directions?" And the teacher showed the boys a piece of plasticine in which four pencils had been arranged to point upwards into diagonal directions.

These were practised freely and individually—some of the boys made a phrase of three jumps into one diagonal direction: others made a phrase of four jumps, one into each upward diagonal: others started with an upright jump and then tipped the second jump into a diagonal, the third returned to the upright, the fourth to a diagonal, etc. These variations were commented upon as possibilities, and the boys asked to become aware of what they, individually, had done. The boys who got most feeling of the daring of the diagonal jumps seemed to land on one foot, although some of them took off from two feet and others from one foot. It was also very obvious that some boys revelled in this off-balance experience, while others felt rather uneasy. The ones who were beginning to master the jumps were encouraged to practise the backward, high, diagonal jumps which had been avoided.

(c) *Contrasts.* The teacher discussed with the boys the contrast between the daring of the diagonal jumps and the aplomb of the dimensional jumps. He then played a record of the Polotsvian Dances from *Prince Igor* for the boys to improvise to, and then to work on in groups of four. They were asked to devise a dance of triumph in which both types of jumps were used.

Some of the groups remained in unison, some split up for part of the dance into two and two, or three and one. There was a tendency for the groups to use the diagonal jumps for travelling and leaping journeys, and the upward jumps for confronting each other. Turning and stepping were freely introduced into the dance sequence in order to emphasise the more important jumping phrases.

Most of the instances given have been of a directed nature, with some opportunities for inventiveness from the boys. Awareness and increasing mastery of the spatial tendencies and possibilities of human movement should also be explored in freer and more creative situations. For instance, any dramatic dance situation can be explored for its spatial characteristics, *e.g.* build a dramatic sequence in twos in which one character moves close to his own body centre, in near extension, while the other character uses movements ranging far from his own body centre, in far extension. Or, in abstract dance, variations in level, pathway and direction can be experienced expressively alone or in groups.

CHAPTER 4

Relationships

THROUGH our human relationships we grow as individuals, and only as developing individuals are we capable of creative relationships. There is a dynamic interplay between these two capacities—the capacity to form satisfactory relationships and the capacity to be an individual. Dance offers the possibility of experiencing very many situations involving range and variety in relationships.

Range and Variety in Relationships

For some time there has been a marked stress in our schools on individual work, on individual progress, on individual achievement and contribution. We know that children progress at different rates, understand by different means, develop in different ways. We have individual library books, programmed texts, language laboratories, and a choice of sports and outdoor activities to cater for individual tastes. The days of each boy's sitting squarely in his desk facing the teacher all day and every day are over in all but the backwaters of education. In those days the only possible and legitimate relationship was that of the teacher with the class as a unit. This, indeed, is still one valid relationship, but it is only one, and it is limited. The good teacher has a working relationship with his class as a unit, but he also works with small groups of children, and with each individual boy. Nevertheless, the whole area of relationships of children with one another, as well as with the teacher, is left haphazardly to chance in most of our schools. True, the well-adjusted boy has no difficulty in forming relationships with his fellows in the school setting, but even these could be extended. For the majority of boys considerable help is necessary, but is not yet adequately provided.

Other people's relationships are discussed in literature and history and divinity, and the good teacher will enable his class to enter imaginatively into these relationships. In games attention is paid to both the competitive and the co-operative aspects of relationship, and the co-operative aspect is also stressed in gymnastics and, again, in some arts and crafts where murals or models are constructed. From conformity and competition we have progressed to co-operation: we have, on the other hand, laid great stress on the individual's private world in writing and painting. We suggest that in creative dance there is great scope for the exploring of individuality and of varied relationships.

In creative dance a boy can have the tangible feel of relationships. He can move alone and feel (1) the reality of his separateness and independence and individuality, but he can also know (2) the reality of being part of a large group that moves as one body, and (3) part of a small group that interacts with other small groups. A boy can experience (4) the different rôles that each individual has in each group—as the tail end of a line, the flank of a moving wedge, the central part of an advancing block or the edge of a whirling mass. He can feel (5) the very essence of two-ness or three-ness that has nothing to do with $1 + 1$ or with $1 + 1 + 1$, but rather the belonging to a new organism that has different powers and potentials from those experienced by the individual alone. The decision and clarity needed to be a leader are learned in movement situations, as is the sensitivity required of two boys who mirror each other's improvised actions. Sometimes conformity to another boy's motif is required, at other times a response that is relevant, or the solution of a problem of movement. Situations constantly change from the conflict of opposing movements to the harmony of a circling mass, or the accurate timing of a group in canon.

There is no rigid line of development in this work because, of course, the whole personality is involved in relationships and we all have different "blind spots." We need to work at establishing a sense of "me" dancing alone, but this cannot be mastered without encountering someone else. It is one of the paradoxes of life that we can only exist fully in relationship with others. Also, we are only able to form relationships with others when we have some personal identity. Different individuals find different types of relationship easier to establish than others. In work in schools, it is obviously important to try to offer a range of situations for relationships, so that each boy can find security in those that come easily to him, and challenge and extension through those he finds more difficult.

Specific Examples of Relationships

The following suggestions are illustrations of movement experiences that seem to help an awareness of the situations involving relationships mentioned at the beginning of the chapter.

I. AN AWARENESS OF SEPARATENESS, INDEPENDENCE, INDIVIDUALITY

(a) *The pulse.* Feel the throb of your own pulse by holding your wrist or temple or neck. It sometimes helps to concentrate if the eyes are closed. Beat the heel in time with the pulse and then begin stepping to the beat. Step out. When you feel secure in the rhythm, release contact with your pulse but keep stepping. After a time find your pulse again and check that you are on the beat. Focus all your attention on your own pulse and your own stepping. Make a triangular pathway on the floor, taking the same number of steps for each side of the triangle. Try this both holding your pulse and without holding your pulse. Enlarge the triangle as much as possible, keeping the beat. Now hurry round the triangle by taking two steps to one pulse beat—twice as many steps round as before. Linger round the triangle by taking only one step to every two pulse beats—half as many steps as before. Choose which side of the triangle will be marked by normal, pulse-beat steps; which will be hurried; which will be lingered over. Do it sometimes holding your pulse to make sure the timing is your individual timing.

(b) *Breath control.* Be aware of your own breathing as you stand. Hold your breath for three counts when I signal and then continue breathing:

    now—two—three—

    now—two—three—

Try this to five and ten counts.

Take a deep breath, then travel to a new place in the room as you exhale and arrive crouching near the floor. Rise to your feet as you inhale, and repeat the travelling and rising to your own breath rhythm. Make the whole body expand and spread as you inhale, and then gradually shrink as you travel and sink. Now develop the rising and spreading into a turn as you inhale.

Try jumping during inhaling and during exhaling. Try rolling also. Make a sequence during three intakes of breath and three exhalations.

(c) *Muscle control.* As you stand, grip every muscle in your body—hold it firmly—and release the tension. Repeat this. Grip towards the centre of your body and release away from it. Grip so firmly that the release moves you to a new spot—then grip again. The release moves you only for as long as you need to regain energy for the next grip. The gripping holds you solidly on the spot. Be aware of the tightening and loosening in your muscles. Now reverse the sequence so that action takes place during the firmness, and the release occurs on the spot. Muscular leaps, turns, rolls, and steps are then contrasted with moments of muscular release in stillness.

2. THE EXPERIENCE OF BEING PART OF A LARGE GROUP THAT MOVES AS ONE BODY

(a) *Group awareness.* Groups of eight, nine or ten stand together with each boy gripping the shoulder of one other boy, so that the whole group is connected. Take a common front in the starting position and build, from stillness, a swaying that takes the group from side to side or from forward to back. Make this swaying build up and die away. Do not push ahead nor hold back, but move with the group. *See* that you are in time with everyone in front and to the side of you. *Feel* that you are in time with everyone behind you. Go on making the swaying build up and die away until everyone is contributing to it and there is no dead weight, no blockage to the unison of the swaying. Now, break away from the group, stay alone and leap into the air and beat into the floor in contrast to the swaying. Don't even look at anyone else as you enjoy your own rhythm of leaping and beating. Return to the group, tune in to the group swaying—attend to everyone else's movement and contribute to the united movement of the sway. Listen, watch, feel, and move with the group. Try this with everyone facing a different way so that the sway will be a forwards-backwards one for some boys, a sideways one for some, a diagonal one for others. Try it also with eyes closed so that the shoulder contact becomes more important, and try it with eyes open, but no shoulder contact.

In order to meet the demands of this situation, there must be individual breakaway periods, as described, when a boy concentrates on himself and his own choice of movement in contrast to the discipline of the group in unison. This is in the nature of the contrasting periods of action and recovery described in Chapter 2: we often intensify one experience by placing it in contrast to another, different experience.

(b) *Advancing and retreating.* The group forms a circle so that each individual can see each member of his own group. Without speaking, begin stepping slowly into the centre of the circle and out again, keeping the steps synchronised. Watch everyone. Develop the rhythm of the stepping so that your group can move as a growing and shrinking circle. When you have developed a group rhythm, try to maintain the circle with your eyes closed.

(c) *Rising and sinking.* With the group bunching together and crouching near the ground, make the group rise in unison to its full height and then sink back to the floor. Everyone together. When this has been mastered, individuals "pop up" from the ground in turns so that never more than one person is moving. Then the unison of rising and sinking begins again.

(d) *Fist-shaking.* Each group forms a mob in which isolated fist-shaking first of all breaks out, and builds into a common fist-shaking that intensifies until the group rushes to a wall and beats on the wall. Do this until exactly the same thing occurs each time and the group rhythm has been formulated and can be repeated.

(e) *Different group shapes tend to produce different patterns of movement.* Let the boys form group shapes and find out what "properties" these shapes seem to have.

3. THE INTERACTION OF SMALL GROUPS

In this situation, the unity of the small group must be established along with the awareness of and response to the other groups. The following is one example of what might happen.

(a) *Wedge, circle and line.* Three groups of five work together in one half of the room. Group A forms a wedge and travels across the room, grazing group B as they pass. Group B revolves, as a result, in a spinning circle as group A passes by. Group A continues to travel towards group C, which spreads into a line confronting group A. Meanwhile group B has spun into a large circle, which encircles groups A and C. Practise this until the groups are moving as units and have developed their rhythms of travelling, spinning into encircling, spreading into a line. Then continue to develop this pattern. These three group actions can first be tried separately—the travelling

51

wedge, the spinning circle and the expanding line. It is hoped that the boys would discover other ways of using these ideas.

(b) *Rhythmical interactions.* Each small group faces inwards on itself, and by the clicking of fingers, beating of heels, or slapping of one's thighs develops a group rhythm. Keeping the rhythm, the group changes its shape from an inward-looking circle to a wedge, a line, a crescent, etc. Keep the rhythm and move to it as the group shape changes. Take the rhythm into the steps and gestures of the body, so that the sound can be dispensed with yet the rhythm remains. When this has been achieved, pay attention to the other groups in the room as well as your own. Notice how your sequence of changing group shapes fits in with those of some other group. Repeat this until you know exactly how your group interacts with this other group. The rhythm that has been built can also carry the group into the general space of the room, and then a change of shape can occur. Movement patterns of this kind cannot be preconceived, and herein lies their value. The teacher must get the initial absorption within the class and then use what evolves. It is wise to repeat before they become too long and complicated.

4. DIFFERENT ROLES WITHIN DIFFERENT GROUPS

(a) *Follow the leader.* In a file, boys follow a leader who determines the method of travelling and the pace, and who is the only one with a clear view of where the file is going. The leader is responsible for the route and for the boys behind him. He must pace his steps or jumps so that the followers can remain in formation; he must take the file through gaps between other groups and around other groups, so that collisions do not occur; he must think ahead and be aware of the length of his "tail". Each boy in the line must watch the boy immediately ahead of him. Obviously it will take longer for boy number five to adjust to any change of step or direction than it will take the second boy. Each boy must try to pick up changes quickly and so keep the file intact.

All these coaching points are quickly learned if the line sets off travelling and then, at intervals, each leader drops to the back of his own file. In this way each boy will experience each situation in the "hierarchy" of a file.

Boys can discover how to change the method of travelling of the file when they are leading it. They can find out the best distance apart for each member of the file. They can make a sequence in which each boy in a file of five leads in his own style, and in some way dissolves the formation of the file after each leader.

(b) *The wedge.* In a wedge the whole group is able to focus on the leader. In a wedge of six the leader is backed by two boys who are backed by three

    *   boys. Establish the feeling of a travelling wedge by making

   * *   "arrow-shots" across the room. As one wedge arrives, another

 * * *   wedge shoots off. Be aware of the power and concentration

given to the leader by the wedge formation. Practise turning the wedge into position for the next "shot" without destroying the formation. Here the outer flanks move through much larger arcs than do the boys nearer the centre of the group. Eventually, during the turns, make a new spearhead emerge so that each boy takes a different part in the formation.

(c) *The block.* In a block of nine or sixteen the front three or four are the obvious leaders, but even they have to synchronise with each other. The focus of the block can of course change, and different leaders can take over.

 * * * *   To get the feel of the block, build up a side-side sway, then a

 * * * *   forward-backward one, then a diagonal forward-right-back-

 * * * *   ward-left, and a diagonal forward-left-backward-right. During

 * * * *   these phrases of swaying, watch, listen, adjust. Keeping the

block formation, work out a floor pattern that takes you forward three steps, to the side three steps, backwards three steps, and to the side three steps so that you have completed a square floor pattern. Do not speak—go on stepping until the block is moving in unison. Do not stop, but keep adjusting and fitting in with the group. Go on until you make it work. Each boy must accept responsibility for his part. Everyone must watch and listen and feel in the muscles the rhythm of the stepping. Some people will have to increase their pace, others will have to slow down. Keep alert to adjustments in the group. It is important that the boys change their positions in this formation from time to time, in order to realise the different demands made. Some of them will feel more secure in the centre of the block, while others will feel confined. The outside edges of the block will make some boys feel free, and others exposed. This formation can be used in dance—for the march of implacable armies, for political demonstrations, for ritual processions of state or religious significance.

(d) *The whirling mass.* Here, again, there is a marked difference between being on the outside edge and completing huge orbits, and being in the centre where one is rotating on the spot. We have tried this in the following stages:

(i) Each boy standing in a space, alone, and whirling and stopping first to a signal and then without a signal. In the latter instance, the whole class must watch each other, so that the whirling begins and ends in unison—as a self-controlled unit.

(ii) In bunches of approximately ten, the *group* turns around once, as a group, and not as individuals. Immediately it is obvious that some boys have to travel through a large circle while others turn on the spot. As the group whirls, each member of it must relate to the centre of the group, by watching carefully, in order to keep it welded.

WORK IN TWOS

There is no end to the number of activities in which an awareness of working in twos can be brought about, and this is merely a selection of some we have tried.

(a) *Moving together facing one's partner.* This demands careful observation of and attention to one's partner and an adjustability in one's own movements. Boys must be constantly encouraged to "watch your partner—don't take your eyes off (say) his feet—stay with him—don't push ahead and don't hang back—you are both responsible for making the two an effective unit." (See Plate 26.)

These same coaching points will be used in the following activities:

(i) Confronting a partner—bounce up and down together—both "upping and downing" at the same time. Do not speak. Then make the bounce die down together so that you achieve stillness in unison. Take a few breaths and then try to begin the bouncing together. Work out, in action and without words, a phrase that begins in stillness, grows to big bounces, and fades away. Perfect synchronisation must be worked for.

(ii) Confronting a partner with the palms of the hands facing the palms

54

of your partner's hands and about three inches apart. Remain in this mirroring situation as you sink down onto the floor and rise high into the air. Can you remain exactly opposite as your hands move apart, and spread and rise, etc.? Watch your partner's hands all the time.

(iii) Confronting a partner, about two yards apart, watch his feet and begin stepping together and back again. Do not stop, but make your steps exactly fit, so that you both begin the advancing and the retreating with the same feet. Bring out the rhythm of the stepping so clearly that you can perform the activity with your eyes closed.

(iv) Confronting with palms facing (as in (ii) above), turn around once so that you finish as you start. Time the turn so that you and your partner both arrive back at exactly the same moment, and with your hands accurately placed. Repeat this so that you are taking the same number of steps around or pivoting together.

(b) *Moving together when partners are not confronting.* This is more difficult, obviously, because neither partner can see the other as easily.

(i) Stepping side by side presents a problem, because couples have not only to synchronise with each other, but to avoid other pairs and the confines of the room. The inside partner has to hold back a little when corners are turned, and the outside one has to step out more. Couples can develop this stepping into a jogging, or even into a rhythmic phrase containing jumping.

(ii) Two boys can make a stalking sequence together—involving rolling and creeping steps with turns and, finally, pounces. Then they might work out how they can start together, each go off stalking alone, and return together at the end. (See Plate 10.)

(c) *Moving alternately,* at its simplest level, is experienced in the following circumstances:

(i) When a class has worked out (say) individual comic sequences based on jumps, and then the class divides into twos. Partner A performs, then partner B, so that each boy alternately performs and then recovers before his next performance. The stillness which is a recovery must now be made more positive.

Watch your partner carefully so that you can start your sequence at the very moment he finishes.

Remain absolutely still while your partner moves, in order both to intensify his sequence and to intensify your sequence. Even when this co-operation and sensitivity have been achieved, there is no real relevance between the sequences A and B as they were worked out independently and simply put together in an arbitrary way. Couples can be given the problem of finding a relevance in the same way in which relevance between disparate objects is found in a collrge.

(ii) When partner A moves while partner B is still and watching, and then partner B copies what he has seen, there is more demand made on both boys. Boy A has to perform clearly and repeat his sequence accurately, and boy B has to observe carefully in order to be able to perform. The alternating phrases should continue until partner B is producing a replica of partner A's phrase.

(iii) Even more demands are placed on the participants if, in reply to a statement of a movement by partner A, partner B has to "agree with" this statement in his own particular way. Partner B must retain something of the flavour of the original statement, *e.g.* its mood; the fact that it contained many changes of level; its rhythm; the predominance of jumping turns, etc. This means that partner B must be responsively alert to A's sequence.

(iv) Similarly the responding partner can be set the task of "disagreeing" with the original statement. Boys will, at first, think that it is sufficient if the replying sequence is performed with a facially antagonistic expression. They have to observe their partner's actions, rhythms and pathways in order to produce a contrast to them. (See Plate 24.)

(d) *Co-operating in a piece of movement.* This is clearly illustrated when boys are given operational jobs to mime in twos, *e.g.* wall-papering, with one person pasting and the other hanging the paper; emptying dustbins, with one boy dragging or rolling the bin and the other lifting and tipping the bin: picking the road surface and shovelling the debris into a barrow. In each case the efficiency of the job depends upon the co-operation of the two boys. The actions of pasting, lifting, digging, etc., must be clearly performed by the body. The rhythms of the actions must be brought out. The placing of tools, soil, bins, etc., must be done with care. Eventually the boys will be able to notice the moments that are key ones to the efficiency of the operation.

From situations like this, the rhythm of the operation can be abstracted, and then used as a starting point for a sequence of movements in which the two boys work in unison or in the same relationship as they had in the mime.

6. WORK IN THREES

Work in threes presents different problems.

(a) *The solo/trio motif.* All three gather round a common centre, seeing that each is equidistant from the centre and from the other two boys. Make a motif that stresses this, *e.g.* stepping around the centre; or towards and away from it. Each boy must watch the other two and keep with them. This unison motif can be broken away from, with each boy leaping on his own and then returning to the trio.

Popular music structured in four-bar phrases makes a good framework for such short dances:

phrase 1: unison
2: individual
3: unison
4: individual

Or each boy can perform his own sequence alone and then all unite on the fourth phrase.

(b) *The solo/duo motif.* If the three boys start together, in unison, and then leave the group in turn, and return to it for the unison motif as a sort of refrain—then we have a very complex change of relationship. There is the "we are a three dancing together," and the "I am dancing alone and unconcerned about the others," and there is also "we are a two that moves differently from a three and from a soloist." It is important in this sort of dance to work out accurately the solo motifs, the duo motifs (three different ones) and the common trio motif in unison.

It will be seen that some boys are very uneasy in one or other of these situations—are unable to work independently and clarify their solos; or unable to co-operate with two people at the same time in the trio, because they seem able to focus only on one person at a time; or unable to work in a duo because they feel compelled either to dominate or to accept the

E

domination of the other. The teacher can help these boys a great deal by drawing general attention to the changing situations of relationship. Coaching points that need to be stressed for these boys are:

(i) always watch and listen, but do not talk, so that your whole attention is concentrated on the feeling of the movement;

(ii) start the movement small so that you have less to adjust and then make it bigger as you and your partner(s) gain confidence;

(iii) repeat and repeat the movement until it is established;

(iv) allow the rhythm within the movement to develop.

(c) *Dramatic sequences*. Interesting, short, dramatic sequences can be worked out by trios of boys on topics such as:

(i) the chase;

(ii) the underdog or scapegoat;

(iii) changing allegiance.

7. DRAMATIC POTENTIALITIES IN GROUP WORK

Further dramatic situations can be explored by individuals and by groups of varied sizes (See Plates 4–7, 27). Some suggested themes are:

(i) Loneliness and isolation on the one hand, and acceptance and integration into the group. This theme would provide obvious opportunities for exploring personal and social problems, problems of the "outsider," "minorities," etc.

(ii) In contrast, the individual's emergence from the group: his expression of confident identity in isolation.

(iii) The challenging of authority: the acceptance of authority, the acceptance being either reluctant or enthusiastic. Again this could be explored in personal (*e.g.* family), social (*e.g.* school or work) or political situations.

It is important to stress, again, that people do not necessarily develop individual confidence and then sensitivity, in twos, threes, fours, etc. There is no systematic progression. Some boys will experience greater security, initially, in a group of five or six, while others will find partner work more congenial. Success in any one situation will tend to give confidence and a sense of security for working in other situations. Consequently the teacher must vary the situations in which he places his classes. He must also recognise that each relationship makes its own particular demands: it is just as important to be able to follow as to lead: it is just as important to be able to work with others as to work alone. We need a wide range of sensitivity to relationships if we are to function adequately in a world where rôles are not so rigidly defined as in the past.

Relationships in dance are not legislated for by apparatus or competition or rules. All such situations are there to be explored—different sized groups, different forms of groups, different rôles within groups. The situations can be freely legislated for by teachers to meet the needs of particular individuals or groups of boys.

CHAPTER 5

The Practicalities of Dance Teaching

THIS chapter will deal with issues that seem to merit special attention for the inexperienced teacher. Some of them have been running like threads through the previous chapters and in the illustrations of work with boys, but they demand emphasis if the teacher is consciously to improve his teaching of dance.

At a simple level one of the most noticeable differences in technique between teaching dance and teaching any other form of movement is the importance in the first instance of working and getting the boys to work in *repeated, rhythmic phrases*. Repetition is an accepted way of becoming familiar with any experience; it ensures that the participant has time to become absorbed in the experience, "to get its feel." The need for repetition can be seen in young children in all their activities: adolescents and adults also need repetition in order to gain the satisfaction of mastery. In athletics, for instance, the repetition of certain movements brings about greater neuro-muscular co-ordination and results in greater efficiency of performance. In dance the repetition of movement phrases enhances the rhythm inherent in the movement, and intensifies its meaning and expression.

A phrase of movement is organic, and ensures that a coherent movement statement is made rather than an isolated action or series of actions. The performer can be helped to employ his efforts in the best possible way over the phrase by being made aware of the length of the phrase and the stresses within it. For example, a phrase may be an even one of, say, five bounces on the spot followed by a pause. In each of the bounces, therefore, the same amount of energy will explode into the air as the body is lifted to the same height off the ground. Because of this evenness, the phrase of five jumps will have a controlled and measured expression, and possibly one of restrained power. Or, in another phrase, the five jumps may increase in size and energy from a very small first jump to a very large fifth jump. To do this, the performer is called upon to manage his efforts differently and, in such a phrase, there would tend to be an expression of mounting excitement. Or in another phrase, the biggest jump may occur at the beginning, and from then on the size and intensity of the jumps become smaller and smaller —then the expression of the phrase is that of an impulsive, impressive start that ebbs away. In yet another phrase, the climax—in this case the biggest jump—may come in the middle so that two bounces would lead into the main, stressed jump, and then the last two bounces would fade away from it: this balanced increase and decrease within the phrase gives a different expression.

Within the simplest phrase is stress and non-stress, accent and non-accent, action and recovery. There is relatedness of one movement to another or to the stillness. There is also relatedness of one simple phrase to another simple phrase.

Teacher Participation

The initial participation of the teacher will often accelerate the process of stimulating a class in dance. This is particularly necessary with older boys and adults, who will invariably feel self-conscious about the activity at first. It will also give confidence to the inexperienced teacher if he commits himself to the warming and mobilising movements at the beginning of a lesson. The following is given as an example:

(a) The teacher takes up the starting position with the class as he briefly explains the position, *e.g.* "Feet astride; weight evenly carried on both feet; fists firmly clenched at waist height in front of you; in an attitude of readiness to go."

(b) As he shakes his hands loose and grips them back in the starting position, the teacher says "Shake—and grip."

He repeats this several times as the boys join in with the action, and he keeps up the accompanying words "Shake—and grip."

(c) As both he and the boys keep the phrase repeating and repeating, he begins to coach them in the movement, within the same rhythmic accompanying framework of "shake—and grip," for example:

"Fingers shake—fists grip."
"Wrists shake—knuckles grip."

"Away from the body—back to the centre."

"Easy release—firm hold."

(d) *The teacher should have provided enough security for the class,* by this time, and focused its energies and attention on the movement, for him to be able to stop moving, and concentrate on observing and coaching. As the boys continue, he must draw their attention to the participation required in the rest of the body:

"Grip in the knees and seat as you grip in the fists."

"Release the hand and neck and shoulders as the fingers shake loose."

"Contrast the free, releasing, expression of the shake with the restrained and powerful gripping."

The following illustrations are all of a warming and mobilising nature. Naturally the body has to be limbered before demands are made on it, and the physical bending, stretching and twisting, and combinations of these are required in dance as in all physical activities. But, hand in hand with these physical actions, the inner efforts of the class have to be aroused, and their attention and concentration focused on the movements themselves.

Coaching

Coaching has to be given just as assiduously as in any other aspect of movement, but it has to go beyond the attention to bodily technique only and concern itself with *coaxing* out the quality that is already latent in the movement. It must bring it to a coherence that is satisfying to the boy. When the movement is directed, as in these examples, then the coaching points are introduced as follows:

EXAMPLE I

Starting position—feet astride with even distribution of weight. Rubbing and kneading the hands firmly together—see that both hands are active and both back and front surfaces are used—then grip the hands together with inter-locked fingers. "Rub—and grip."

Then involve the shoulder girdle in the action and finally the spine, so that the body winds firmly around—twisting and circling on its base.

"Wind—and pause."

EXAMPLE 2

Beating the feet quickly into the floor with a stabbing,

"ra—ta—ta—ta—ta—ta," pause,

"ra—ta—ta—ta—ta—ta," pause.

Allow the heels to touch the ground during the pause, then beat with the balls of the feet. Keep the body compact with its weight over the feet; ease the muscular tension during the pause.

Then alternate the stabbing feet with a pause in which the body is held balanced on the balls of the feet. During the pause the body will then lift a little, and spread as it eases and prepares for the next beating. (1) and (2) can also be performed simultaneously, so that the upper half of the body is winding while the lower half of the body is beating. This needs practice and concentration to master.

EXAMPLE 3

Starting position, standing with weight on right foot. Shake the foot and ankle of the left leg, then step to the left side with it, releasing the right foot. Shake the right foot—step sideways and press it into the ground.

"Shake—and press."

Make the shaking occur far out to the side of the body, and then step to the same side, so that the pressing step makes the hips scoop through a U-shaped pathway before the other foot is released. Grip in the hips during the pressing step.

Carry the top of the head high and spread and lift the arms a little to assist balance.

EXAMPLE 4

Starting position with feet together and palms of the hands together. Rub the palms of the hands firmly and quickly so that the friction generates warmth—then spread them away from each other slowly—and begin the quick friction again as the hands re-unite. Fingers should be together during the rubbing, and then spread apart as the hands spread and circle back together. The friction should be firm, followed by quite gentle spreading through the air. Feel the heat of the friction and the dissolving of it during the spreading.

The body will be compact and gathered in a slightly crouched position during the rubbing, and then spread as the hands and fingers part. Make the spreading happen in the chest also. If one side of the body spreads further away than the other and describes a larger circle, this circle can be enlarged still further by turning around with a few steps. A complete sequence would be:

(a) both hands rub and spread symmetrically on the spot;

(b) both hands rub, but the right side then leads into spreading and turning;

(c) both hands rub, but the left side then leads into spreading and turning;

(d) repeat (a).

EXAMPLE 5

With the weight of the body supported on the left foot, hold the right foot off the ground on the right of the body and slightly forward. Relax the ankle and foot, and then slap the sole of the foot against the floor as it is drawn towards the supporting leg, lifted towards the knee, while the hip should also be relaxed. Emphasise the circular motion of the action. Repeat three times on each leg. Build a phrase that increases the size of the circle. Carry the body upright. Finally perform this circular slapping of the foot while hopping on the other foot.

EXAMPLE 6

With feet astride, spread the arms sideways at shoulder level and carry the head high. Pull apart the two sides of the body—feel the pull in the sides. Drop the body down between the knees, as they bend and the arms sweep across the floor, crossing each other. Then swing the arms outwards again as the body lifts into the starting position.

"Swing and drop—swing and lift."

"Seats down and knees turned out."

Let the head drop and lift with the curling and straightening of the spine.

The swings described by the hands should be semi-circular.

Let the weight of the body drop into the swing, then capture a

PLATE 25

An example of moving together, but not in unison. The boys established contact and each had then to adjust constantly in order to maintain contact whilst moving. Here was a careful interlacing of fingers; other boys maintained a firmer grip. After moving together, the boys broke away from each other and danced alone before returning, like the pair in the background, to the sequence of moving together.

PLATE 26
The boys tried to build rhythmic phrases of jumping in twos. They mirrored each other's movements as they intensified the elevation and then diminished it. The synchronisation with a partner demanded a gradual development of the phrase with clear effort expression and this in turn demanded bodily control in throwing the body into the air.

PLATE 27

A dramatic sequence in which a group is developing detail through definition: "How heavy is it?"
"What is it?" "Show the answers in your body."

From left to right, the first and fourth boys show concentrated expression in their bodily attitudes
and this is carried through into the finger tips. Both boys hold themselves on different bases. The second
boy showed a general care and sensitivity but this was not carried through into his stance. The third
boy concentrated his energy in his neck and head and produced little power in his hips and legs.

PLATE 28

The aim here was to bring the group to rest with a common focus. The illustration shows the end of a humorous dance invented by the boys. There was little evidence of bodily skill but the spirit of the group indicated the pleasure gained by the boys from working in group situations that give scope for the comic interpretation.

moment of suspension as the body is lifted and spread and held.

There is a small, resilient bounce near the ground as the swing changes direction from crossing to spreading.

EXAMPLE 7

The upper half of the body can be swung across and around the lower half. Take up a starting position with feet astride, but with the weight more on the left foot than the right, as both arms reach towards the left. As both arms swing in front of the body and over to the right side, the weight is transferred across. The upper half is twisted at the waist on the lower half.

"Swing—and swing—and swing—hold."

"Follow the pathway of the hands with the eyes, so that the head swings with the movement."

"The hips remain fixed and forward while the shoulder girdle rotates."

"Increase the intensity and size of the third swing so that the body is turned around."

"Swing—and swing—and swing into a turn."

So far, the lower half has simply accompanied the swing through weight transference—now make the legs drive away from the ground during the third swing, so that the body is lifted off the ground as well as turned.

"Swing—and swing—and swing round in the air."

EXAMPLE 8

Swings of the legs, with the upper half of the body accompanying the action, also help to mobilise the often rigid pelvic area in a rhythmical way that leads very easily into steps and jumps.

Take the weight on the left foot and reach forward with the right foot so that it extends forwards at about knee height. Carry the head high and the arms spread to give balance.

See that the back swing is as high and as far away from the body as the forward swing. Out-turn in the hip and the knee of both the supporting and swinging legs.

The third swing can lead into a step, close, step before the other leg begins to swing.

There should be a resilience in the body and especially in the supporting leg during this sequence.

Similar swings of the legs can cross and swing away from the body, both in front of and behind it.

EXAMPLE 9

Stand upright, with feet together. Lift the heels off the ground so that the weight rolls forward onto the balls of the feet. Let down the heels. Regulate this action by breathing in as you lift high, and breathing out as you replace your heels on the floor. Lift the chest as you inhale.

Press downwards into the floor as you exhale, and grip in your seat and knees; release the tension as you rise. Bend your knees—right down—as you press into the floor, and release high and spread and hovering. The release can then be taken into either turning or leaping or both.

Work Devised by Class: The Questions to Ask

The absorption of the class will be harnessed only if the coaching points, some of which are exemplified in (1)–(9) above, arouse the energies and focus the attention of the class on the performance of the movement itself rather than on mechanical action. Then the phrases will become meaningful and expressive.

These illustrations should demonstrate that quite unambitious movements can begin to provide dance-like experiences. The examples given can be varied by:

(a) Changing the parts of the body being used, by placing the action somewhere else in the body, *e.g.* in the shoulders instead of the hands.

(b) Changing the stress within the phrase as explained at the beginning of this chapter.

(c) Changing the level or direction or extension in space of the action.

In the previous examples the movement experience has been directed by the teacher. When movement sequences have been devised by the boys, how then can the teacher help? The easiest way is through *verbal questioning* that prompts movement clarification. Note that the class *does not reply verbally, but in movement.*

The three parts of a phrase of movement that have to be clarified are, obviously, the beginning, the middle and the end. But it is suggested that the middle—the main action itself—is clarified first, and then the preparation for it and the result of it. Each of these three sections could be clarified in each of the four aspects of movement (refer back to Chapter 1), but some questions will be more appropriate in some situations than others.

Of the main *movement event* we can ask:

(a) What action takes place and which parts of the body move?
(b) How does the body move?
(c) Where does it move?
(d) What relationship has this event to the whole phrase or series of phrases, to the environment and to other people?

Of the *starting situation* and the *resulting situation* we can ask:

(a) What is the position of the body and its parts?
(b) What attitude and energy are apparent?
(c) Where is the body in space?
(d) What relationship has this beginning and end to the whole event?

More detailed questioning on the four aspects of movement may now be given. It is suggested that the teacher will select questions relevant to his lesson from the following list.

1. THE BODY: THE NATURE OF ITS MOVEMENT

(a) What *activity* does the body perform? Does it travel, turn, leap, gesture or remain still? In *travelling*, is the body carried on hands, feet, or some other part(s)? How many steps or rolls are taken? In *turning*, is one side of the body wrapped across to make a closing turn, or is one side flung sideways to make an opening turn? Which side initiates the turn? Which foot is used as a pivot? Or do the feet take small steps around on the spot? What is the amount of turn? Is it one complete revolution or a half turn or a three-quarter turn or two and a quarter turns, etc.? In *leaping*, is the take-off from one or two feet? Is the landing onto one or two feet? Which, therefore, of the five basic jumps is used:

    both feet to both feet,
    both feet to one foot,
    one foot to the same foot,
    one foot to the other foot,
    one foot to both feet?

Is the body carriage held during flight, or does the body move in the air? Do the chest, head, spine and arms assist the propulsion from the legs and feet? In *gesture*, which parts of the body move and which are held? In *stillness*, what supports the body, and how is the rest of the body related to this support?

(b) Which *parts of the body* are most active or important in the movement? Which parts initiate or lead? Which support and carry the body? How are these parts assisted by or related to the rest of the body?

(c) Is there an *asymmetric* (one-sided) stress in the body, or are both sides of the body used together in a symmetrical way?

(d) Is there a *successive* (travelling from part to part) or a *simultaneous* (taking place in several parts together) flow of movement through the body?

2. EFFORT: HOW THE BODY MOVES

(a) Does the movement happen in one sweep or in several sections?

(b) Where is the climax or are there several climaxes?

(c) What is the nature of the dynamics of the movement? Does the movement remain firm or delicate throughout or does it alternate between the two? Does the movement show changes of time—sudden flashes of action and periods of sustained leisure? Does the movement focus directly and go straight there, or does it meander flexibly? Does the movement "stream out" or is it restrained?

(d) Are there any pauses? Is the body held firmly or gently?

3. SPACE: WHERE THE BODY MOVES

(a) Does the level of the movement remain the same throughout or are there changes of level?

(b) Does the direction of the movement remain the same throughout or are there changes of direction?

(c) Does the movement take place near to the body or far away from it?

(d) Does the movement travel through the centre of the body or peripherally round the centre?

(e) What patterns does the movement make in the air and on the floor—in curved or angular or twisted forms?

4. RELATIONSHIP

(a) Are you alone and concerned with your relationship to your own body, the dynamics of your movement and the relationship of yourself to the space?

(b) Are you concerned with your relationship to another person, a trio, a small group or a large group?

(c) What is the nature of this relationship? Is it one based on actual physical contact that might be firm or might be gentle? Is it one based on synchronisation and timing? Is it one based on being part of a pattern or formation together? Is it one based on an easy moving in sympathy, or on careful control?

(d) Do you meet, part, move together with or deliberately avoid your partner(s)?

Selection of the appropriate question at the appropriate moment is a skilled part of the teacher's craft. Too few questions, or questions that are not demanding enough, will fail to help the boys to reach a satisfactory and satisfying standard of achievement: too many questions will merely confuse and dishearten.

These and similar questions can provide a valuable and much-needed check for the teacher at certain stages of a course. He will be able to evaluate the improvement of individuals and of groups of boys. In what aspects of movement do they show more awareness and sensitivity and skill and range? Which aspects has he, as the teacher, given priority to (because of his own personality and preferences), and which aspects has he neglected?

It can be seen that such questioning and clarifying contributes considerably to *progression* in dance. There is no linear progression: we cannot enumerate the steps of becoming articulate in the expression of movement any more than we can systematically produce artists in other fields. Progression is essentially individual, and the teacher has to be sensitive to the moments when boys need the security and re-assurance of being praised about what they have produced already, and the moments when they need encouraging beyond the bounds they have set themselves. Progression will take the form of greater range and clarity and mastery of all aspects of movement, and each boy can only proceed from what are clearly, already, his own characteristic movements. In creative work, progression can be assisted by the tactful teacher, but does not depend on his direct intervention. Indeed this can hamper creative work if used insensitively. It is the teacher's skill as an enabler which will ensure progression. As with teachers who are concerned with other art forms, the teacher of dance must have the capacity to assist the boy to imagine more intensely, and to realise more vividly and clearly, the experience he is trying to communicate. Though understanding of the nature of movement contributes to this, the confidence inspired in the group, and the atmosphere of enthusiastic acceptance of ideas and experiment that has been generated by the teacher, are of fundamental importance also. In such an atmosphere, individuals may achieve results which go far beyond what they had expected of themselves, or the teacher anticipated for them. Such results may be spasmodic, but the experience of them will extend the limits of potential, and will heighten aspiration.

There are teachers who can stimulate a richness of creative work that is very exciting for boys—for a time. There are teachers who can logically and systematically train craftsmen in movement. The dance teacher must do both.

Index

J

RE